# BASEPATHS

# BASEPATHS

## *From the Minor Leagues to the Majors and Beyond*

MARC GUNTHER

*Charles Scribner's Sons · New York*

Chapter 1 of this book appeared in *The Sun Magazine,* a section of *The Baltimore Sun,* on August 21, 1983.



Library of Congress Cataloging in Publication Data

Gunther, Marc, date
Basepaths : from the minor leagues to the majors and beyond.
1. Baseball—United States. 2. Baseball players—United States—Biography. I. Title.
GV863.A1G86 1984 796.357'0973 84-13881
ISBN 0-684-18175-4



1 3 5 7 9 11 13 15 17 19 F/C 20 18 16 14 12 10 8 6 4 2

*Printed in the United States of America*

# Acknowledgments

I am grateful to many people who helped me with this, my first book. My editor, David Toberisky of Charles Scribner's Sons, helped shape the idea for *Basepaths* and then encouraged me to write it. I am indebted to him for taking a chance on an unproven writer.

I would also like to thank my agent Ellen Levine, Claire Smith, Leslie Sharpe, and the staffs of the New York Yankees and New York Mets. Warren Goldstein, Steve Metcalf, and Gerald Kleiner provided helpful suggestions with the manuscript, and Don Heiny, who took many of the photographs in this book, was also a good companion.

Irene and Irv Weinstock, Ed Gunther, and Andy Gunther were as supportive as any family could be. I owe special thanks to Noel Gunther, who read every word of the work in progress.

Finally, I am fortunate to be married to a woman who is a fine editor as well as a wonderful wife. Karen Schneider read and edited several versions of *Basepaths* before anyone else got a look at it. She also put up with me, cheerfully, through nearly two years of reporting and writing. This book is for her.

# Contents

# Introduction

*Basepaths* is a book about baseball players and their careers. Some of the players are famous stars, some are unknown, and most are somewhere in between. Each was chosen to represent a stage of a baseball career, from beginner to retiree.

The book begins with the story of Mark Heyison, 21, a hopeful but unproven third baseman who has just left college to start his pro career in the lowly Appalachian League. It ends with Jim "Catfish" Hunter, 38, who was once a celebrated pitcher and is now a soybean and peanut farmer in his native North Carolina. In between are stories of several minor leaguers, a rookie, a journeyman, a star, an aging veteran, and an ex-player who chose to stick with the game by becoming a broadcaster.

These players have at least one thing in common. They were willing to talk with an ordinary fan—me—about what it's like to play baseball for a living. They talked, not only about life in the big leagues, but about playing baseball in school and in the minors. They talked about their insecurities as well as their dreams, their frustrations as well as their successes. They talked, in particular, about the most interesting question of all: how they mastered the game of baseball.

I soon learned that making it to the big leagues and staying there demands a lot more than the ability to hit, throw, and field a ball. It takes a special kind of character.

No single word can explain what's required. Some players call it determination, while others say the key is confidence. Some talk, in near-mystical ways, about maintaining intensity and staying relaxed at the same time. The ability to overcome severe injuries preserved the careers of several players in this book.

But whether you call it good competitive instincts or mental toughness or perseverance or simply desire, baseball players who have reached the top of their game share a special quality. The mind, clearly, is as important as the arms or legs in determining a player's fate.

Different stages of a career pose different kinds of challenges. For a beginner like Marc Heyison, the hard part is ignoring the odds. He probably won't make the big leagues, but he must not think of himself as a long shot. He can't afford to become discouraged.

For Ron Kittle, a slugger in his rookie season with the Chicago White Sox, hitting home runs was easy. But he also had to cope with the strikeouts and severe batting slumps that destroy many young hitters. He needed an inner strength, as well as a powerful swing.

Ferguson Jenkins of the Chicago Cubs, a veteran of 18 seasons in the big leagues, says he still learns something new every time out. Unlike so many pitchers who must quit when their fastballs lose their zip, Jenkins has hung on. His knowledge of the game has made the difference.

Hardest of all, perhaps, is saying good-bye. Bill White, an intensely competitive man who fought his way to the top as a player, found that he was a beginner all over again in his new career as a broadcaster. Catfish Hunter had to choose between his love of baseball and his deep attachment to his home town when his playing days ended.

By the time I finished my work, I found that I had written about more than baseball. These are stories of people learning to cope with new challenges and to adjust to changes in their lives. Because they happen to be baseball players, they must face challenges and make changes that are as dramatic and unpredictable as the action on the field.

But the path from the minors to the big leagues and beyond is, finally, not much different from the paths we all travel as we move through the stages of our careers and lives. The obstacles are familiar; the qualities needed to overcome them are the ones that bring success in any undertaking. *Basepaths* is about baseball, but it is also about the pursuit of excellence. These are stories of people who are striving to be the best at what they do.

This book is based on interviews from the 1983 season, with the exception of Chapter 2, which was written in 1982. An epilogue written in June 1984 brings the players' careers up to date.

EARLY INNINGS

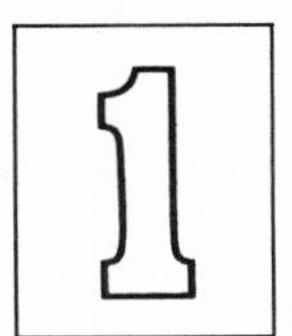

# Beginning: A "Baby Bird" Learns to Fly

As the bus carrying the members of the Bluefield Orioles struggles over the last of the Appalachian Mountains and finally pulls into Calfee Park in Pulaski, Virginia, Marc Heyison has the jitters.

It is Opening Day of the 1983 baseball season in the Appalachian League and Heyison, a twenty-one-year-old infielder with the Orioles, is about to play his first game as a professional baseball player. He is beginning a difficult journey of his own—one he hopes will carry him to the major leagues.

The Bluefield players and their opponents, the Pulaski Braves, line up for introductions and traditional pregame ceremonies. They look like a couple of high school or college teams, and, in fact, most of the players are barely out of school.

"During the national anthem, I was real nervous—thinking about how I was going to do and all," Heyison says later. "I was thinking about what was going to happen to the first ball I got."

It doesn't take him long to find out. In the first inning, Heyison is playing third base for Bluefield when the first Pulaski batter hits a hard bouncing ball right at him. He clutches it to his chest and fires to first for the out.

"That was something," he says, smiling, the next day. "I'm kind of glad that happened, because after that . . . I relaxed a lot more. Fortunately, it wasn't that difficult a play."

What follows is a typical night of baseball in the Appalachian League. With enthusiasm if not finesse, the teams plunge into a messy contest of strikeouts, walks, errors, and wild pitches—too many events to jam onto the tiny scorecard sold in the ballpark. The game seems to last forever.

But if the baseball, like the players' uniforms and the outfield grass, is a little ragged, that is to be expected. The Appy League is a Rookie League, and most of these players are teenagers playing baseball for a living for the first time.

They are measuring their skills against those of their teammates and awaiting the chance to prove that they have what it takes to succeed in professional baseball. They know that only a lucky few will reach the top. But for hundreds of young men who have dedicated themselves to a single goal—playing baseball in the major leagues—this is where it all begins.

The hilly backcountry of the Virginias, Kentucky, and Tennessee has been home to the Appalachian League since 1911, when, long before television, big crowds would turn out for games. The Baltimore Orioles have had their rookie team in Bluefield, a town of 16,000 people on the Virginia–West Virginia line, since 1957. The team is called the Orioles, and somewhere along the line someone nicknamed it the Baby Birds.

Bluefield is a city in decline. With the coal industry slumping, the acres of railroad yards that were once the city's commercial heart are quiet. All that's left downtown, since a big mall went up nearby some years ago, are a grimy bus station and a couple of fast-food joints. One of the main thoroughfares is called Bland Street, and the name fits.

Still, for Marc Heyison, who comes from the pleasant suburban town of Silver Spring, Maryland, there could be no better place to spend this summer of his twenty-first year. Heyison is a clean-cut, nice looking young man with brown hair, brown eyes, and a boyish smile. On the baseball diamond, he is a hustling, talk-it-up type of player who plays with intensity. Off the field, he is quieter and more serious than many of his teammates. He is pleased to have this chance to play professional baseball and determined to make the most of it.

Heyison has been a baseball nut and a fan of the Baltimore Orioles since he was a kid. His father, Harold, went to high school across the street from Memorial Stadium and has been rooting for the Birds since they played in the International

League. Harold was an athlete himself, earning all-state honors in high school basketball and later competing in a tough fast-pitch softball league. He remembers that Marc, even as a youngster, would toddle along with him to any sports event.

"We'd go along to the softball games and he'd be running and throwing and catching with everybody," Harold Heyison says. "He'd be a bat boy and everything else."

Even as a youngster, Marc worked hard at sports. "He just kept plugging away," his father recalls. "He would practice, practice, practice, and he'd just keep on getting better each year."

At Springbrook High School, Marc played baseball and basketball and piled up impressive statistics in both. He hit .471 during his senior year and began to attract some attention from scouts. But when the Cincinnati Reds offered him a contract after a tryout, he turned them down, electing to go to college instead.

"I wasn't getting any money. Even the scout was honest with me and said I'd be smart if I went on to get my education," Heyison says.

While Heyison was offered baseball scholarships by several colleges, he chose to attend George Washington University in Washington, D.C., mostly because it was near home. Heyison also liked the baseball coach, Jim Goss.

Goss describes Heyison as a quick learner with lots of natural talent: a strong arm, surprising speed, and hitting ability. "He picked up immediately on anything I worked with him on. He was very intelligent," Goss says. "Unquestionably, he has the right kind of attitude."

Heyison's best college season came in his junior year, during the spring of 1983. His batting average of .461 was good enough to rank him twelfth among the nation's collegians, and he was second in the country in triples. He was considered an excellent fielder, too.

"He put on one of the most awesome hitting displays that I've ever seen," Goss remembers. "He just went on a tear that didn't stop."

Still, there was some question about whether Heyison would be chosen when the major league teams gathered for the annual draft of amateur talent early in June. The June draft is the main source of young talent for big league clubs, which spend considerable time and money scouting players before making their selections. About nine hundred players are chosen from a pool that includes all the high school seniors and college juniors and seniors in the country.

Doubts about Heyison's attractiveness stemmed from two factors: his size and his choice of college. Heyison, at 5 feet 9 inches, is smaller than most professional athletes, and he is a bit chunky at 180 pounds. (The Baltimore Oriole roster is dominated by six-footers, though outfielder Al Bumbry is just 5 feet 8 inches.) Heyison doesn't appear sleek enough to be a speedster or strong enough to be a power hitter.

On top of that, George Washington is not the kind of college that turns out professional ballplayers. Its baseball schedule consists of thirty-five to forty games, half as many as the baseball powers in the South and West play, and the level of competition is not as high. The 1983 season had been a washout in every way. Games were rained out, postponed, and never played, and the team's record—it finished with 7 wins and 25 losses—attracted few scouts.

So, when the season ended in May, Heyison made plans to spend the summer playing ball in a well-regarded amateur league on Cape Cod and to return to school in the fall for his senior year. Then the scouts began to call—seven or eight of them, most just to get acquainted. Two—Jim Gilbert of the Orioles and a scout for the Atlanta Braves—called to set up individual tryouts.

One morning early in June, Heyison, Gilbert, and Jerry Small, a second scout for the Orioles, met at the baseball field of Howard University in Washington. Gilbert, an Oriole scout for eight years, hadn't seen enough of Heyison during the season to judge his talent. The two scouts watched as Heyison took batting practice and fielded ground balls, and they timed him as he ran the bases. Gilbert says the tryout is one way of testing a lesser-known player in a pressure situation. "We take them there to see if they're sound, just like a race horse. You find out what they can handle."

When the tryout ended, Gilbert told Heyison that he liked what he had seen. Still, Heyison was not certain that he would be drafted, so he proceeded with plans for a summer on the Cape.

On the afternoon of June 7, he was halfway to the Cape—he had stopped at his girlfriend's house in New Jersey—when his brother reached him with the news: Baltimore had chosen him in the ninth round of the draft and was prepared to offer him a contract. "I just couldn't believe it had finally happened," Heyison remarks. He decided, though, to think things over for a couple of days. Signing a professional contract would automatically cancel his college baseball scholarship and perhaps make it harder for him to finish school. "It was a tough decision," he admits. "I really want to finish up. That's the number one thing. I want to get my degree."

The same day, in small towns and big cities across America,

two dozen other young men were being called by parents or friends or scouts with similar news from Baltimore. The 1983 edition of the Bluefield Orioles was beginning to take shape.

Wayne Alan Wilson, seventeen, was sitting in his fourth period nutrition class at Redondo Beach High School in Redondo Beach, California, when the school principal walked in with a surprising announcement. Wilson, a pitcher, had been the first player chosen by the Orioles.

Michael Conley, eighteen, a pitcher, was at home in Hamilton, Ohio, when he learned that he had been picked in the second round.

Randy King, eighteen, was in Tulsa, Oklahoma, hoping to play baseball rather than go to college. He went in the fifteenth round.

Dan Fitzpatrick, nineteen, a catcher, was at home in Baltimore. The news that he had gone in the twenty-sixth round was especially sweet since Fitzpatrick had been cut from his high school team twice. He finally made a team and gained notice in junior college.

Thousands of miles away on the island of St. Maarten in the Caribbean Sea, Edward "Tony" Rohan had a unique problem. As a foreigner, Rohan, seventeen, was not subject to the draft. He had agreed to sign with the Orioles but was now struggling to get a visa to enter the United States.

Heyison, meanwhile, made up his mind to sign, deciding it was time to test his skills in the professional ranks. Baltimore ended his worries about college by offering him a bonus that would cover his last year of tuition. He could spend the summer in Bluefield and return home in the fall to resume work on his degree without worrying about finding the money to pay tuition. (Neither Heyison nor the club will say how much his bonus was, but middle-round draft picks usually get about $5,000 to sign.)

"I've been rooting for the Orioles since I was a little kid. That played a big part in it, too," he says.

Baltimore eventually signed nearly all of the twenty-nine players it drafted. Most would wind up in Bluefield, though some would be assigned to the Newark (N.Y.) Orioles, a Class A team in the New York Penn League that was also beginning its season in late June. (The Rookie League, designed for beginners, is a notch below Class A. No more than ten players on a rookie team roster can be over twenty-one, and none of the players can have more than two years of experience. No such restrictions exist in Class A.) For now, though, all the draftees —whose lives would soon become nearly as regimented as those of military inductees—were given plane tickets to Miami, Florida. At the Orioles' minor league training complex on the campus of Biscayne College, where they would train for about a week, they joined players who had signed as free agents, were chosen in a previous draft of amateurs, or were returning from a season in the minors.

In Florida, the emphasis is on fundamentals. Upon arrival, each player is handed a four-hundred-page loose-leaf book outlining the ways the team will respond to every game situation. Some of the players grumble that they just left school and now have to start studying all over again.

Like companies in any business, baseball organizations develop their own philosophies and styles. The Orioles, who have compiled the best record of any major league team in the past ten years, are known for the importance they place on developing players in the minor leagues. They have built their championship teams not by trading or signing expensive free agents, but by carefully nurturing the talent in their minor league system. Players are taught the game from scratch—and in precisely the same way—at every level of the organization from the low minors on up to the big leagues.

Len Johnston, an executive-level scout with the club, is in charge of spring training for all the Oriole minor league teams. He says the organization, more than most, emphasizes the importance of fundamentals and team play.

"We start off right away on pickoffs and rundowns," he explains. "The way a pitcher picks a runner off, the right way for the first baseman to chase a runner toward second, the way the shortstop covers second and comes off the bag to make the tag. We get that down pat so we know what everyone's doing at all times."

The players practice fundamentals every day in Florida, and will continue to work on them all summer. Even on days when a game is scheduled, Oriole teams will devote a couple of hours in the morning or afternoon to drills.

They study pickoffs, rundowns, bunts, defenses against the bunt, outfield relays, base-running, stealing, ways to organize hitting and fielding practice, even how to warm up. The players are told that there is one way, and one way only, to do all these things, and that is the Oriole way.

Learning the game anew has a leveling effect on the team. "Some of these kids come from a little high school where they've had an easy coach and they're the big deal," Johnston says. "The college kids might come from a small college where they actually ran the team. Some of the college kids might want to strut their own stuff. But we have a way of getting around that and making them come around to our way—how we want to teach them."

This sits fine with Heyison. He enjoys basic baseball and willingly spends time memorizing the book of plays. He is also smart enough to learn all the variations without much trouble.

Having watched the Orioles over the years, he knows that a team that can execute the fundamentals has a good chance of success. "That's the way you've got to start," he observes. "That's the most important part of the game. If you can do that, then everything falls into place."

As a third baseman, Heyison plays a key role in many defensive plays because he relays the signals from the manager in the dugout to the other infielders. On bunts, for instance, Heyison's signs tell his teammates who should charge the plate and who should cover which base.

There is, off the field as well, an Oriole way. Dress codes are enforced. Portable radios, except for those with headphones, are banned from the clubhouse. Players must wear their caps at all times on the field but are forbidden from wearing them outside the ballpark.

"It's just little codes and you figure, what's that got to do with playing good baseball? Well, everything we do has a meaning," Johnston says firmly. "We let them know what to expect, what to say, what not to say. We represent the Oriole organization, and we're proud of that and go accordingly."

Some of the players chafe under the new regimen, and one or two defy it openly, sporting their caps around town or playing radios when the manager or coaches aren't around. Perhaps in a reaction to the discipline, or perhaps because they are a typical bunch of eighteen- to twenty-one-year-olds, some of the players become pretty rowdy away from the ballpark.

First in Florida, and again in Bluefield, there are nighttime trips to local bars and expeditions during the day to beaches, shopping malls, fast-food joints—anywhere girls might be found. The players get to know each other and fall into the patterns of horseplay and teasing that seem to be part of sports.

Soon many of the players have nicknames—Blackie and Fitz and Pizza-man. Billy Ripken, eighteen, an infielder and younger brother of Oriole shortstop Cal, is simply Rip. This is his second season in Bluefield; because of that and his ties to the big leagues—his father, Cal Sr., is a Baltimore coach—he emerges as a team leader.

Rip is also the team's leading smart aleck. He keeps up a constant stream of chatter around the batting cage. "Was that a swing you took?" he says incredulously to catcher Frank Lopez. "I've seen better swings on a porch." Lopez is a chunky, good-natured fellow, and because of his lack of speed afoot, he earns a humorous nickname: Slow-ped.

Heyison does not have a nickname, and though he is as much a part of the team as anyone else, he does not spend time in the bars or cruising for women. He has a girlfriend back home, and besides, he is older than most of his teammates. He goes along with the discipline without much fuss.

"The biggest thing they look at is your attitude," Heyison says. "I personally feel that everyone down here is as good as you are, so good ballplayers are a dime a dozen. If you have the right attitude, it's bound to help."

In addition, Len Johnston—a gruff, craggy-faced man in his forties who patrols the practice fields with a clipboard and barks out commands to the players—is not the kind of man nineteen- and twenty-year-olds tend to talk back to. "We tell them, you can't argue too much about our way," Johnston says. "All you have to do is look at the record."

The week in Florida passes quickly, and it is time to head north. Getting to Bluefield is an ordeal: the players pile into a bus for an eighteen-hour overnight ride with just a couple of brief stops. They are stiff and cranky when they arrive.

Unhappiest of all is Wayne Wilson, the team's top draft pick from California. He missed the week of training in Florida to graduate from high school and was flown to Miami on the last day of camp. While he could have flown directly to Bluefield, team officials said they wanted him to ride the bus so he could meet the rest of the team. "That was a killer," Wilson grumbles. "It was really terrible." He is 6 feet 3 inches and 180 pounds, uncomfortably large for a bus seat.

Heyison isn't bothered as much—his body is better suited for bus travel, and he learned to sleep on bus trips while he was playing in college. When he couldn't sleep, he read a long historical novel.

The bus pulls into what might be the prettiest spot in Bluefield—Bowen Field, the home of the Baby Birds. The ballpark is cradled between two steep hills: one behind home plate, where the stands are built right into the hillside, and the other, lined with tall trees, beyond the outfield fence. The trees stretch high into the sky to form a perfect dark green background for hitters (pitchers don't like it). The field itself is well-maintained, and it looks inviting and ready for play.

The baseball has to wait. For now, the players, tired as they may be, begin looking for places to live. The Orioles will put them up at a motel for two nights, but after that they are on their own.

There is, however, help available from several people: George Fanning, Bluefield's longtime general manager; Len Johnston, who is traveling with the team for a couple of weeks; and Greg Biagini, the rookie manager. If the Baby Birds were a family—and sometimes they seem like one—Fanning would be the grandfather, Johnston the father, and Biagini the big brother to the players.

Fanning's strong suit is practical know-how. He has lived in the area all his life and has run the team for twenty-nine years, so he knows everyone who has an apartment or room to rent to a player. "Some of them get nice places and some of them get damn ratholes," Fanning says.

Fanning also handles the team's finances, including the payroll. Since the players won't get paid for two weeks, he obliges a couple of them with advances on their salaries. Players in their first season in Bluefield are paid $600 a month, plus $11 a day for meals when the team is on the road.

A burly man in his seventies, Fanning is also the unofficial team historian. He has been a coach, manager, groundskeeper, and concessionaire to teams in Mercer County since the 1930s (the Bluefield Bluegrays were a Boston Red Sox farm club back then), and he likes to reminisce about Appy League legends like Leo "Muscles" Shoals, a 1940s slugger who was compared to Babe Ruth. Fanning has seen hundreds of players come and go.

Johnston, who was a stern taskmaster in Florida, now assumes a more protective role. He establishes the team at a local motel where the rooms cost $18 a night, checks with players each day to see who has found apartments, and arranges rides to the ballpark. When Tony Rohan, the seventeen-year-old from St. Maarten, finally gets his visa and plane ticket, Johnston goes to tiny Mercer County Airport to welcome him to the Orioles—and to the United States.

The older man's soft side shows through as he talks about the adjustments these players are making. "It's the first time they've been away from home. It's the first time they've been in Florida. It's the first time in Virginia. It's the first time for a lot of things," Johnston remarks, raising his eyebrows and glancing knowingly over at the sideline where some teenage girls are waiting for the players to finish practice. "They come in here from all different places and they talk all different languages. You got the Boston twang and the New Jersey accent to the North Carolina and the Texas drawl. Everybody should be on the staff of a Rookie League club. It's an experience and a half."

Greg Biagini is only thirty-one, but he is a veteran of the minor leagues. He spent ten years as a player—the last five in the Mexican League, where his goal was to earn enough money to put his wife through college. Then the Mexican economy went sour, and he quit. "They were talking about paying in pesos, and pesos don't buy much up here," he explains. One of his old managers helped him land the managing job at Bluefield.

For a 6 feet 2 inch, 205 pound former college football player, Biagini exercises his authority gently. Sometimes he will loosen up with players before a game and join them in batting practice. There is plenty of kidding when he steps into the batting cage, swings at a pitch, and misses. Nearly everyone calls him Skip, short for skipper.

"I feel personally that you have to be their best friend, their father, their mother, their big brother, and their manager," Biagini says. "They have to do everything on their own now. They can't count on anyone, like Mom or Dad, to be there. They have to do their laundry, cook, whatever."

While Heyison has lived away from his family before, the campus at George Washington is less than an hour's drive from his home. He is used to having his parents attend all his games and seeing his girlfriend regularly. His parents and his girlfriend plan on visiting during the summer.

In Bluefield, Heyison teams up with George Page, a twenty-one-year-old outfielder returning to the team for a second season. They find a small apartment—one bedroom each, a kitchen, and a living room—in Princeton, a couple of miles from the ballpark. They will travel to the park with two players who live nearby and have a car. (Three other players chip in $100 each and buy a battered 1973 Chevy Impala, which they show off proudly.)

Like most of his teammates, Heyison isn't particularly concerned about finding a nice place to live since he figures his stay in Bluefield will be short. He is eager to move up, even before his first season as a pro has begun.

"My parents and everyone else I talk to at home say not too many people get an opportunity to do this, but I really don't consider it that big a deal," Heyison says. "I mean, I'm glad I got the chance and everything. But I won't say I accomplished something unless I make the major leagues."

The number of players who began their careers in Bluefield and went on to play in the big leagues sounds impressive at first. Without much provocation, George Fanning will give you the list.

"Mark Belanger was through here. Boog Powell was through here. Dean Chance, Doug DeCinces, Eddie Murray, the shortstop Ripken," he says. "You've got Sammy Stewart who came through here, Davis came through here, Grich, Baylor." He can't possibly remember all the names; fifty-two Bluefield graduates have gone on to the major leagues.

It sounds pretty good, that is, until you realize that those fifty-two players were spread over twenty-six years of rookie ball in this town, or until you consider how many players started here and failed. Just a couple of players each year—if that—will rise to the top. No one bothers to keep track of those who don't, but the number is probably close to seven hundred.

Some players find out in a hurry that they don't have the right stuff. Roughly half will play no more than two seasons in the minor leagues before being cut. Last season, nine players were released in midsummer. The clubhouse was somber after the nine were told to pack their bags and go home.

Steve Spalt, twenty, a shortstop from Baltimore in his second season in Bluefield, remembers saying good-bye to the players that night and giving silent thanks that he was not among them. "If you mess up a lot, you know you might get released any second," he says. "I worry about it a lot."

It can, however, take much longer for a player to find out whether he has the ability to make the majors. After a season in Bluefield, players typically get promoted to the Class A team in Hagerstown, Maryland. The AA Charlotte (S.C.) Orioles represent the next rung on the ladder, and the Rochester (N.Y.) Red Wings, classified AAA, are a step—albeit a giant step—below the big leagues.

The Oriole philosophy is to bring players along slowly, and even good players are usually given three or four years of minor league experience before making the big club. Other players spend eight or ten years moving slowly up through the minors before they realize that they will never make it. They leave the game or try again—as Biagini is now doing—as a coach or manager. Johnston spent fifteen years in the minors before ending his playing career.

The Bluefield players try not to think about such things, and they seem ill at ease when forced to talk about the long odds facing them. Different players have different ways of coping with—or ignoring—the fact that their chances of making the majors are slim.

Spalt says the worst thing you can do is worry. "If you do worry a lot, you might screw up. There's a lot of pressure in this game." Yet he recognizes that he may fail and forces himself to attend junior college in the off-season, where he is studying accounting as a backup.

Tony Burroughs, an affable nineteen-year-old pitcher from Baltimore, thinks the competition makes it harder for players to get close to each other. The Bluefield team is carrying fourteen pitchers on its roster, and some are certain to be cut in midseason.

"You want to have friends," Burroughs says. "But everybody's out here trying to do a certain job. You're aware there's a competition."

Others are more sanguine. Rohan, the first player ever signed from St. Maarten, seems sure that he will also become the first player from his island to reach the major leagues. "I know I'm going to make it," he says, matter-of-factly. "You've just got to put your mind to it." He won't even discuss the possibility of failure.

Heyison is more realistic, perhaps because, at twenty-one, he is one of the more mature players on the team. His maturity is, in some respects, an asset; it makes it easier for him to accept team rules and adjust to life away from home. But when it comes to making the major leagues, his age is probably a strike against him. For one thing, major league organizations have higher expectations of players signed out of college than they do of those who just left high school. The Orioles are likely to be more patient with the weaknesses of a seventeen- or eighteen-year-old who has had less time to develop and has more time left to improve.

Heyison fidgets a little when asked if his age creates pressure on him to move up in a hurry. "Sure it does," he says finally. "But I try not to think about it too much."

He has, however, set a rough timetable for himself, giving himself three or four seasons to move up. "If I'm in Triple A [the highest level of the minors], I'd probably stick it out for a couple of more years. If I was in A ball or maybe Double A at that age, I would. . . ." He won't come out and say the word "quit." Then he adds, "I can tell if the handwriting's on the wall. I'd just as soon get back to school and get my degree."

It's clear after just a couple of Oriole workouts that if Heyison doesn't make it, it will not be for lack of trying. He works hard at what he does. (His father says, "One thing I always stressed to him: you don't have to be a good player to run on and off the field.") Heyison also seems to take every part of the game seriously—more so than many of his teammates.

The Orioles, for example, enjoy a batting practice ritual called "Hits." Each player steps into the batting cage and gets to swing at one pitch. If the ball is driven into the outfield for what would be a base hit, the player can keep swinging until he makes an out. Naturally, this gives rise to good-natured arguments over whether a batted ball is actually a hit and to competition over who can last longest in the cage. Even Biagini takes his turn.

Heyison isn't really part of the joking. A right-handed hitter, he stands in to swing with his elbow and bat held high in the air and well back—a picture of concentration. When he tops the ball and hits a slow grounder, ending his turn, he walks a few steps away to work on his timing or refine his stroke. He will scowl or kick the dirt if his performance displeases him, even during practice.

Baseball is no longer just a game for him. It is his everyday work, and Heyison, for the first time, is playing for keeps. This change—the fact that the players must come out and perform every day—is said by coaches to be the toughest thing about moving from high school or college into the professional ranks.

"It's definitely a big adjustment," Heyison agrees. "You have to get used to doing baseball day in and day out. Plus it all counts.

"The coaches don't put the pressure on you," he goes on, "but I feel a lot of pressure. You've got to perform. I try not to put too much pressure on myself, but I don't like to screw up too much."

Determination is, of course, essential to baseball success. But Heyison must also guard against trying too hard. During batting practice on the afternoon before Opening Day, Heyison was having problems in the cage, popping up several pitches in a row and then tapping a couple of weak grounders. Biagini noticed him pressing and called a halt.

"Stay back. Keep your hands back," Biagini told him. "Hit down on the ball." Biagini later explained that Heyison had been too eager to hit the ball and was lunging at it rather than waiting to drive it back toward the pitcher.

At such moments, the odds seem to be preying on Heyison. It's been said that 90 percent of baseball is played from the neck up, and for these rookies it may well be true. They must be able to deal with the contradictions of life in the minor leagues. On the one hand, the players have to be realistic about the odds against them, if only to prepare for the likelihood that they will fail to make the big leagues. Yet they must also go about their work without feeling too much pressure, and with the confidence that they will succeed. It is difficult to hold onto both these attitudes at once, but Heyison tries.

"I'd be lying if I said I didn't want very much to play in the major leagues. I believe I can play in the major leagues," he says. But he adds, "I don't have all my marbles banked on making it. If I don't make it, I'll have to adjust. It'll be a hard adjustment, but I'll have to do it."

There is a magic to Opening Day, even in Pulaski's Calfee Park—a rundown spot in a nondescript town about an hour's ride from Bluefield. The outfield is lopsided, the infield is lumpy, and the wooden stands could use a fresh coat of paint. This is fairly typical of conditions in the Appy League. In the ballpark in Paintsville, the sun sets over the outfield fence at an angle that makes it impossible to hit for a few minutes, so night games are often stopped for a brief "sun delay" during the early innings. The schedule also requires an innovation, known as "split doubleheaders," where one home team plays two different visiting teams in a single evening.

The fans at Calfee Park have a reputation for being tough, and some of the people who show up on Opening Day soon demonstrate why. They boo mistakes on the field, and a couple of burly men in T-shirts yell racial taunts at the black players. The distance to the field is only a few feet, but the players show no sign of hearing the insults.

Otherwise, this is a typical minor league crowd—small (911) but surprisingly noisy, composed mostly of families with children and older people. General admission is $2, but children and senior citizens pay just $1.50. The program is full of misprints—Heyison somehow came out Agyson—but the popcorn is hot and fresh, and some fans wash it down with a drink known locally as a "Suicide"—three-quarters Coke and one quarter Sprite. Country music is played through loudspeakers between innings.

The players, who have been preparing for this game for days, are eager to get started. For many, like Heyison, it will be their first taste of professional baseball, and while seventy-one games will follow this summer, this one will probably be remembered best by those who play in it.

Not that the game itself is particularly memorable. The pitchers on both teams are wild, the hitters look awkward, and the fielding is erratic. It is obvious after a couple of innings that Heyison isn't the only young man on the field with the jitters.

Batting eighth in the order, Heyison comes up for the first time in the second inning and is hit by a pitch that glances off his helmet. With two men on base in the third, he hits the ball sharply but right at the pitcher, who throws him out. In the sixth, he pops to third and, on the way back to the dugout, throws his bat down in disgust.

In the field, Heyison is steady, particularly on a key play in the bottom of the sixth when the Baby Birds get to test their ability to execute fundamentals. With Pulaski runners on first and second, they defense a bunt perfectly—the first baseman and pitcher charging, Heyison holding back. When the ball is bunted toward first, first baseman Brad Beattie grabs it and fires to Heyison for the force out. Watching from behind home plate, Len Johnston has a simple reaction: "Super."

The game, meanwhile, is shaping up as a topsy-turvy affair. Pulaski takes an early 3–0 lead, but Bluefield surges ahead in the middle innings, 5–3. Neither team seems capable of holding onto a lead, and when Heyison comes to bat for the fourth time in the seventh inning the game is tied, 5–5.

He soon takes care of that. With Bluefield runners on first

and third, he hits a soft, looping fly down the right field line just beyond the first baseman's reach. His first hit as a pro isn't pretty, but it is timely and he drives in the go-ahead run.

"It felt good," Heyison says later, savoring the moment. "I wish I had hit the ball a little better but it was still a hit. The time before that, I hit the ball really well but right back at the pitcher, so I guess it all evens out."

As Heyison stands on first, Coach Mike Verdi walks over to pat his rear. Heyison tells him, "I can tell my grandkids that my first hit in pro ball was a real shot," and the two men share a laugh.

The smiling continues as Bluefield rallies for three more runs to build a 9–5 lead, which going into the bottom of the eighth inning looks reasonably secure.

But Pulaski won't quit. The Braves quickly load the bases, and a pudgy, right-handed designated hitter named Wayne Harrison steps up. Calfee Park has one oddity—a hill in right field that rises beyond a short fence, just 291 feet from home—and that is exactly where Harrison drives an outside fastball for a grand-slam homer to tie the game. It is the first home run of the season, coming at a perfect time for Pulaski, and the fans make as much noise about it as they can.

With the game tied, 9–9, Heyison leads off the ninth for Bluefield. He takes a couple of hard strikes on the outside corner to fall behind in the count, 1–2, and then lunges and misses a sharp breaking curve that is low and outside. Scowling as he walks back to the dugout, he makes no effort, again, to hide his frustration.

"I struck out on a bad pitch," Heyison explains the next day. "I don't mind striking out if the pitcher throws a good pitch and he beats me, but when he throws a bad pitch and I swing at it, that makes me that much more mad."

When Pulaski comes to bat in the last of the ninth, no team has been retired in order in any inning. With its 20 hits, 19 strikeouts, and 14 walks, the game is nearly four hours old.

It ends quickly, on one more walk and a long drive to the gap in left-center that scores the runner all the way from first and gives the Braves a 10–9 victory. The Baby Birds throw their gym bags over their shoulders and trudge across the dimly-lit field to pile into the bus and ride home.

Heyison is not discouraged by his performance. He had a single in four trips to the plate and, more importantly, felt comfortable with the level of play. "I was expecting it to be a lot tougher," he says.

He seems more relaxed than before, now that his first game as a Bluefield Oriole is behind him, and that raises a new question: What would it be like for him if someday he gets the chance to play his first game as a Baltimore Oriole?

Heyison grins. The subject is one he has thought about before. "That would be pretty special," he says. "If I ever play in Memorial Stadium, I don't know what I'd do on the first day. I don't know if I'd be able to walk up to the plate."

Then a new thought occurs to him. "I think," he says with a broad smile, "I'd probably get a few autographs."

# 2 The Long Road: *Oil Can Boyd and Paul Hundhammer of the Bristol Red Sox*

Oil Can Boyd gets the ball to the plate in a hurry. He has a loose, easy motion as he warms up on the pitcher's mound, pulling his left knee up to his chest, pausing for a moment, then whipping his right arm over the top. His fastball is just a blur in the twilight until it hits the catcher's mitt with a loud *thwack*. Then, flipping his glove over to signal the catcher, Boyd tries a curve. This time, the ball loops toward the plate over a wide arc, seeming to travel in slow motion.

Near second base, Paul Hundhammer gathers in a bouncing ball, pulling it toward his chest with both hands. He takes a little skip toward first base and flips the ball smoothly to a teammate. A moment later, Hundhammer bends over to remove a couple of pebbles from the basepath, hoping to prevent a bad hop. Then he turns to check the flagpole near the plate to see which way the wind is blowing.

Oil Can Boyd and Paul Hundhammer are preparing to go to work. They are minor league baseball players warming up for a game, going through the motions that have become the routines

*Paul Hundhammer (left) and Oil Can Boyd*

RED SO

of their daily lives. Their performance in this game, as in every game they play, will help determine whether they will ever realize their goal of playing in the major leagues. As they have dedicated themselves to baseball, Boyd and Hundhammer have become close friends as well as teammates.

Their careers have brought them to Bristol, Connecticut, a sooty industrial city of 57,000 people, and specifically to Muzzy Field, the home of their team, the Bristol Red Sox. It is nearly 7 P.M. on the evening of August 26, 1982, and in about half an hour Boyd and Hundhammer and the rest of the Red Sox, a farm team of the Boston Red Sox, will take the field to play the first game of a four-game series against the Reading (Pa.) Phillies, a farm team of the Philadelphia Phillies.

The outcome of the game doesn't mean much to either team. With a week remaining in the Eastern League season, Bristol has only a slim chance of making the league playoffs, and Reading has no chance at all. But to individual players, the contest is important. Their successes and failures will be reflected in the season's statistics, and their play will be observed firsthand by the group of major league scouts who sit in judgment behind home plate. The scouts all have clipboards and pens, and they take notes even during warm-ups; one also has a "gun" to measure the speed of Boyd's pitches.

Boyd and Hundhammer will get special attention from the scouts because they are considered prospects, which means they have a chance to play in the big leagues. Not all minor leaguers are prospects. Some are older players hanging on, hoping to get a coaching or managing job, and others are players needed to fill a spot on a roster.

Boyd and Hundhammer came to professional baseball in very different ways. They grew up in opposite ends of the country, and if it weren't for baseball, their paths never would have crossed.

Boyd, who is twenty-one, comes from a large family of poor blacks in Meridian, Mississippi. His father and uncle and brothers all played baseball, and the game came naturally to him; as a youngster, he displayed great skill as a pitcher. Boyd still approaches the game with all the enthusiasm of a young kid who has yet to discover the limits to his talent.

"I feel special. I really do," he says. "Everything I've ever wanted to do on a pitcher's mound, I've been able to do."

Hundhammer is a Californian. His family is middle class and not particularly sports-minded, though he played sports as a kid because it seemed like the thing to do. He was a good athlete but never a star, and it wasn't until recently that Hundhammer, who is twenty-four, thought he might be able to play in the big leagues. His determination, as much as his natural ability, has carried him this far.

"It's like I'm a late bloomer," Hundhammer says. "It's like the girl in high school who's skinny, and she's got big lips and nobody likes her and everybody calls her an ugly duckling. Then they turn around and they see her at the ten-year reunion, and she's the prettiest girl that's there and everybody wants to dance with her."

Boyd and Hundhammer both signed professional contracts in 1980. Since then, they have managed to survive the weeding out process that takes place in the lower levels of the minor leagues: the Rookie and Class A leagues. The Eastern League is classified as Class AA, or Double A—roughly halfway up the ladder that forms organized baseball—and Bristol is the second highest ranked team of the five teams in Boston's minor league system.

"It's a major accomplishment to get here," says Edward M.

Kenny Jr., Bristol's general manager, who can usually be found before a game sitting in the tiny cubicle behind home plate that serves as the team's office. "Anyone who's made it to Double A ball would be at the top of his profession really, if it were any other profession besides baseball."

Boyd and Hundhammer take little comfort in knowing that they are already among the best baseball players in the world. They still have a long way to go to reach the major leagues, and just as they took different paths to Bristol, they have different ideas about how they will make it to Boston.

Boyd is, quite simply, counting on his exceptionally strong arm. He can stand on the left field line near third base and throw a baseball—hard and without a bounce—all the way to the fence in right field. On the mound, he has a blazing fastball and good control of his pitches.

Boyd sounds cocky in a matter-of-fact way when he talks about his ability, and he has no reason to be modest: he is about to finish his third consecutive winning season in the minors. Certain that his talent will carry him to the big leagues, Boyd talks about skipping over Class AAA, the next level of the minors, and playing next season in Boston. When he is asked what he would do if he fails to make the majors, he looks astonished.

"I swear to God that has never crossed my mind about me never making it to the bigs. I would like to play in the show, in the bigs, next year, some kind of way," he says. "I pretty much feel I could be in the show now with some other teams, but Boston may take a little longer in seasoning their players. I want to play for this organization, but I don't want to be over-patient about it. I want to play."

Hundhammer, in contrast, cannot rely on raw talent. While he works hard to make the most of his ability, he lacks the physical gifts of some players. His speed is only slightly better than average, his throwing arm is just fair, and hitting has, at times, been a problem for him.

Nevertheless, Hundhammer believes that he can play in the big leagues, and he is always on the lookout for that extra edge that will help him get there. He has qualities—determination, intelligence, a willingness to sacrifice for his team—that are hard to measure but are valued by managers and coaches. A thoughtful and articulate young man, Hundhammer emphasizes these qualities when he talks about his prospects.

"Statistics are important but a manager is looking for a complete baseball player, somebody that's willing to sacrifice a runner by hitting a ground ball to second base with a runner on second to move him to third, who's going to hang in there on a double play, who's going to root his teammates on when he's not hitting well," Hundhammer says.

"That's the type of player that the Red Sox are looking for. You can get to Triple A quicker if you hit .260 and you're a team player than if you hit .320 and you're an individual," he says confidently. He hopes to be promoted to Triple A next year.

For now, though, Boyd and Hundhammer must call Muzzy Field home. Built in the 1920s, Muzzy is a cozy, old-fashioned ballpark with a covered brick grandstand behind home plate, wooden bleachers along the left field line, and an outfield fence papered over with advertisements. Unlike some minor league parks, where conditions make playing difficult, this one is well-maintained; the grass is trimmed and the lighting adequate. Muzzy seats 3,500 people, and on game nights it is often the liveliest spot in town—all green and bright and cheery, and noisy with fans waiting for the baseball to begin.

The players are supposed to wait in the clubhouse, a dingy

and depressing place that hasn't had a fresh coat of paint in years. The toilets have no seats, the shower area is tiny, and players always seem to be bumping up against one another. Boyd and Hundhammer say their hometown high schools had better facilities. So, along with many of their teammates, they pass the time after their warm-ups and before a game hanging around outside the clubhouse. Some players say hello to fans they have come to know, a few flirt with giggly teenage girls, and some sign programs for youngsters. Tonight, with the season nearly over, one player presents a nine-year-old fan he has befriended with a good-bye gift: a pair of roller skates.

The sky is still light as a scratchy version of the national anthem is played over the loudspeakers. Back on the mound, Boyd hurries through his final warm-ups with an eager let's-get-going look.

For such a hard thrower, Boyd is short and skinny—5 feet 10 inches and 145 pounds, ten pounds less than he weighed when the season began twenty-five weeks and nineteen starting assignments ago. His uniform hangs loosely on him, and his arms and legs, while muscular, are surprisingly thin. He has a long face, a trace of a mustache, and a broad smile.

Boyd's given name is Dennis, but he is known to his teammates and to fans as Oil Can. He picked up the nickname as a teenager in Meridian, where beer cans were called oil cans and Boyd was known for being able to put away plenty of them. The nickname is sewn onto his jersey, and he is sometimes called OC or simply Oil for short.

This game is important to Oil Can. He has 177 strikeouts in 180 innings this season and needs three more strikeouts to break the season record for a Bristol pitcher. Boyd also needs two more wins to reach 15—a milestone in the short minor league season—and tonight and the last game of the season next week against the Lynn Sailors will be his only two chances.

Hundhammer, too, is approaching this final week of the season with intensity. He has done fairly well this summer but thinks he should have done better, and he wants to end the season on a positive note. His season certainly began in the right way. He hit over .300 for the first six weeks and impressed his manager, Tony Torchia, with his fielding. But Hundhammer sprained his ankle in June, missed twenty-two games, and was shifted to a new position, third base, when he returned. He had difficulty adjusting in the field, and his batting average dropped to .270, the lowest, he says, since he started playing pro ball. He wants to improve it.

Now back at second base, Hundhammer is comfortable again in the field. He has sure hands, and though he is a little chunky at 5 feet 9 inches and 175 pounds, he is built low to the ground. He has a short neck, a square jaw, and thick curly brown hair that sticks out from under his blue and red cap.

Like Boyd, Hundhammer has become a favorite of the Bristol fans. One group of fans joked so much about his unwieldy name that they showed up at the park one night with a big sign saying Kepple-Mayer, claiming they couldn't spell his real name. The lettering on his helmet says HUNDY and that is what most of the players call him.

Both Bristol and Reading are young teams, composed of players like Boyd and Hundhammer who are in their early twenties and have two or three years of experience in the minors; the players are neither newcomers nor veterans but somewhere in between. (There are, of course, exceptions. Reading's Richard Wortham, twenty-eight, pitched a couple of seasons with the Chicago White Sox, lost his stuff, and is now trying to work his way back up—without much luck. His record is 0–3.) Typically, the players are eager, optimistic types who believe that they can make it to the majors, even though the odds are heavily against them. Half of the players in this game will probably never even reach the next level of the minors, Class AAA, and no more than a handful of those who do are likely to enjoy major league careers.

The game begins, and Boyd's first pitch is a hard, low fastball for a called strike. Keith Washington, Reading's leadoff man, is a speedy switch hitter who bats out of a crouch, and Boyd feeds him nothing but hard stuff: a fastball outside for a ball, the next one over for a called strike, and then a riser over the plate at the letters. Washington swings at this last one, but much too late, and he is out. Strikeout number 178.

Luis Rodriguez, Reading's next batter, is a right-handed hitter who has bounced around the minors for a few years. He goes down on strikes, and the crowd starts to clap in anticipation of another strikeout. Boyd, looking confident, is working quickly on the mound.

The clapping stops, however, when a right-handed slugger named Paul Fryer steps up and hammers a fastball down the third base line for a double. The next batter, Miguel Ibarra, is a dangerous man—a strong, stocky hitter with home run power. The Reading threat is a sudden reminder that Boyd has been plagued by two problems during the season: run-scoring outbursts in the early innings and the long ball.

"I come out there a little nonchalant about the first inning," Boyd says when asked about the problem. "I give up early runs in the first two or three innings. Then I throw shutout ball through the rest of the ballgame. That has happened to me a lot of times, in rookie ball, college ball, everywhere I play ball. I give up runs early and then I throw blank ball."

Boyd, like most minor leaguers, prefers not to dwell on his weaknesses. If he gives up lots of home runs, well, he tells himself, so do many fastball pitchers. "Any hitter in the lineup can hit a home run off you, throwing the ball like I do. I've given up as many home runs this year on good pitches as I have on bad pitches. And I can tell, when a guy reaches down and away and hits a slider out of the ballpark, hey, that's not my night." He adds a moment later, "A lot of pitchers up there [in the big leagues] give up 40, 50 home runs, and they're the best pitchers in the league."

Boyd mixes up his pitches to Ibarra, who works the count to 2–2. Then Ibarra swings through a slow curve for strike three, leaving the runner stranded at second. Boyd, who is often demonstrative on the mound, slaps his mitt against his thigh and trots off the field. He has struck out the side, tying the team strikeout record, and he seems to be having fun.

Growing up in a family of baseball players in eastern Mississippi, a part of the country where baseball is by far the most popular sport, Boyd was practically reared on the game. His father, Willie James Boyd, who now runs a local nursery, was a semi-pro shortstop, and an uncle, K. T. Boyd, was an outstanding pitcher in the old Negro Leagues. Both played with the legendary black pitcher, Satchel Paige. Three of Oil Can's brothers also signed professional baseball contracts: Steve with Boston, Mike with the Los Angeles Dodgers, and Don with the St. Louis Cardinals. None, however, reached the big leagues or even the Double A level.

"I learned to play from my brothers," Boyd says. "Coming from a baseball family, everyone wants to see you play ball. Your brothers played, you gotta play; that's the way everyone felt."

Soon Boyd dreamed of playing professionally, and he began

to devote himself to baseball. "I played with some good little ballplayers, but guys just didn't desire it as much as I did," he says. "I had my ball and glove with me every day in the classroom, and I would take my ball and glove when I got out of class to go to gym. Everyone else shot basketball or whatever the gym class was doing that part of the year, but my coach would let me play catch with somebody there because I was getting ready to play high school ball."

Even in those days, Boyd had style. He wasn't afraid to let his feelings show on the mound, and he enjoyed performing in front of a crowd. "I always had form and I would say a little bit of finesse with my game," he says. "It's common down that way, hot-dogging on the ballfield and wearing your socks real high. We used to wear elastic in our socks. We'd jack 'em way up." He giggles at the memory.

Boyd was an overpowering pitcher at Meridian High School, where his earned run average hovered around 1.00. At Jackson State University, he won 18 games and lost 5 in three years. "He was the type of kid who didn't believe in being defeated and didn't mind expressing it," says Bill MacFarland, his high school coach, remembering what he called Boyd's "bulging confidence." In the June 1980 draft of college and high school players, Boston chose Boyd in the sixteenth round.

In the bottom of the first inning, Bristol comes to bat to face Leroy Smith, a Reading right-hander who has 9 wins, 5 losses, and more than 100 strikeouts. Smith fans the leadoff man, center fielder Steve Lyons, before shortstop Jackie Gutierrez singles to center. Hundhammer, who bats third in the lineup, is next.

Hundhammer approaches the plate purposefully, digging a small furrow with his spikes and planting his right foot firmly in it. He then places his left foot in the front of the batter's box and wriggles into a deep crouch, with his rear end pointing back toward the dugout. He glances at the pitcher and takes his practice swings, his bat slashing the air. The routine, which he has been through hundreds of times, ends, and he is ready to hit.

Hundhammer is not a natural hitter. He learned hitting, which he describes as a science, by working at it every day for years. The difficulty he had learning to hit almost cost him the chance to play professional baseball.

Born in Hawaii, Hundhammer grew up in Orinda, California, a well-to-do suburb of San Francisco. Through high school and college, he was a good baseball player but never a standout.

"I have never, not on one team that I have ever played on, have I been the star . . . and here I am in Double A baseball," he says with some amazement. "I would say that 95 percent of these guys were *the* stars on the teams that they played on when they were younger. Absolutely.

"I didn't even hit .300 in high school. I went to junior college in Los Angeles and hit .260. My highest average was when I was a senior in college and I hit .282," he says. Hundhammer always played on winning teams, though, and he enjoyed the game so much that he began to consider a professional career.

His best chance of getting drafted and signed by a major league team came after his senior year at the University of Miami. He was a fine fielder, his hitting had improved, and he was named to the all-tournament team when Miami played in the College World Series in 1980. Hundhammer hoped his performance had impressed some of the major league scouts in attendance.

"Right after that, I thought I'd be signed," he recalls. "I

always wanted to be drafted. That was one of the biggest things I wanted so badly, to receive a letter from Bowie Kuhn's office, and it never happened."

While nearly eight hundred players—including Boyd—were chosen that June in the draft, Hundhammer was not one of them. He began to analyze why he had been passed over. "It all stemmed from hitting," he says. "I wasn't really that big. They didn't think I had any power. If I couldn't hit for a high average at that level, what was I going to do when I started facing these pitchers?"

Though Hundhammer couldn't play professional baseball that summer, he played baseball anyway. He joined a college all-star team that toured Europe, hoping for another chance to turn pro.

"People kept coming back and saying, you know, it's just a crime that you weren't drafted. What am I supposed to say, 'I know, I feel the same way but no scout wanted me'? It was very, very frustrating. I wanted to get back in the game very much. I wanted to prove to myself that either, one, I wasn't good enough to play with these guys and it would show, right away, I would be overmatched, or, two, that they made a big mistake in overlooking me."

His break came that fall. Miami's coach, Ron Frazier, persuaded George Digby, a Red Sox scout, to sign Hundhammer to a contract. He was given a small bonus of $1,000 and told to report that winter to the team's spring training base in Winter Haven, Florida.

On this evening, Hundhammer steps in for his first at-bat against Reading's Smith and falls behind in the count, no balls and two strikes. He is a patient and disciplined hitter, waiting for the pitch he wants to hit, even if that means watching some good pitches go by.

"I'm looking fastball most of the time," he explains. "If they throw a curveball for a strike and it's a good strike, down low or on the corner somewhere, I'm going to give the pitcher that pitch. I'm not going to swing at that pitch and make an out. He's going to have to make another good pitch to get me out.

"Every good pitch a pitcher throws, I hope I take. Every mistake he makes—just gets it up a little bit, leaves it over the plate a little bit—that's the ball I want to hit. That's the one I'm looking for."

Hundhammer cracks the next pitch on a line to right center field, and Gutierrez starts digging for second. But the ball hangs up for a moment before it is caught by the center fielder, and Gutierrez scampers back to first. Two out.

The next man up, Reggie Whittemore, is a crowd pleaser, though probably not a major league prospect. Whittemore, who is twenty-five and playing his second season in Bristol, is the best-known player on the team. A powerful right-handed slugger, he likes to swing for the fences until the pitcher gets two strikes on him—a strategy that sometimes produces home runs but more often results in strikeouts. The fans enjoy his free-swinging style, though, and his approach to the plate is heralded by chants of "Reg-gie, Reg-gie" from the stands.

This time, Whittemore connects. He drives a curveball on the outer half of the plate high and hard to the opposite field, and the crowd rises to watch the ball disappear into the trees beyond the right field fence. The Bristol team gathers at the plate to greet him, and Oil Can Boyd, delighted with his sudden 2–0 lead, skips into the air as he slaps Whittemore's palm.

In the top of the second, Boyd is throwing hard—probably close to his top speed of 90 to 95 miles an hour. After retiring the first two batters on ground balls, he goes to work on Joe Nemeth, a big left-handed hitting first baseman. Nemeth takes a strike, pulls a pitch hard but foul past first base, and then swings and misses a fastball for strike three. The public address announcer says Boyd has broken the team strikeout record, and the fans applaud appreciatively as he trots to the dugout.

The record-breaking strikeout is hardly a momentous event —it is witnessed by just 1,633 fans—but it must be considered a highlight of Boyd's brief professional career. After getting drafted by the Red Sox in 1980, Boyd left college to join Elmira in the New York–Penn League, a Class A league populated mostly by players just out of high school or college. He won 7 games and lost just 1, posted an earned run average of 2.48, and struck out 79 batters in 69 innings. That was a fine beginning by any measure, but Boyd feels he should have done better. "If I knew anything about what I know now, I would've won 25 games," he says with characteristic bravado.

His next destination was Winter Haven, home of the Red Sox farm team in the Florida State League—not really a step up, since that league, too, is mostly for newcomers and classified as Class A. Boyd continued to shine, compiling a 14–8 record with 154 strikeouts.

This summer, his third as a pro, Boyd has pitched as well as anyone in the Eastern League. He leads the league in strikeouts and has walked just 45 opposing hitters, surprisingly few for a hard thrower. He has won 13 games and lost 7, and a couple of the losses were low-scoring contests in which his teammates did not give him much offensive support. "Oil Can has not pitched in a game that he could not have won all year," observes Torchia, his manager.

Boyd's task, at the moment, is to learn how to make the best use of his talent. He is trying, for example, to refine his four basic pitches—the fastball, curveball, slider, and straight changeup—by changing speeds or altering the spin on the ball. "I'm just working on making those pitches more effective, like getting the slider down and away. I've always thrown hard breaking balls. Now I've got to learn to take something off it, learn how to pitch a little more," he says. Too often, he realizes, he simply tries to overpower hitters with his fastball, rather than mixing up his pitches to surprise them. He also has a dangerous tendency to go for a strikeout—"to do all the work himself" as the saying goes—rather than to pursue the more effective strategy of letting the batters hit the ball but not giving them pitches they can hit hard.

"Sometimes I become a three-pitch pitcher," he admits. "I get two strikes on a guy and I throw the third one over, which sometimes might be a good pitch to hit. You shouldn't give a guy a good 0–2 pitch to swing at." In baseball lingo, Boyd is more a thrower than a pitcher.

"I think I've just got to learn to be mental, more of a mental ballplayer," he reflects, "because physically I feel pretty solid. I throw strikes and I don't walk people, and I got a real good idea of what I'm doing out there. You don't have to do much thinking when you've got good, exceptional stuff. It gets them out by itself. It makes it a plus when you can think with it, too."

In the home half of the second, Boyd gets a bigger cushion to work with. Juan Pautt, Bristol's designated hitter, leads off with a double and comes home when third baseman Lee Pruitt smashes a home run. Bristol has a 4–0 lead and the PA announcer says that Pruitt, like every Red Sox player who hits a homer in Muzzy, has just won a free pizza from West Side Pizza in Bristol.

Boyd gets into a minor jam in the third, when the leadoff man reaches base on an error by Whittemore. But he strikes out two more Phillies to prevent any real damage. He is firmly in command.

In the Bristol half, Hundhammer comes up with one out and nobody on. For the second time in the game, he hits a solid drive to center field—this one travels farther than his liner in the first—only to watch it be caught. He trots back to the dugout, his lips pursed and his eyes trained on the ground in front of him.

Hundhammer is not as expressive or emotional as Boyd. Both his style of play and his personality are more controlled. Sometimes, though, Hundhammer cannot hide his frustration. He is disappointed in the way this season has gone, especially in comparison to last year, his first in pro ball. He arrived for that first spring training in February 1981 with no guarantee of making a team.

"I came in there a scared little boy," he recalls. "I had a lot to prove, and luckily I had worked very, very hard getting ready and I came into camp in top shape. I was just ready and I took advantage. Plus"—and here he sounds surprised—"the caliber of ball was not as overwhelming as I thought it would be."

He was assigned to Winter Haven, where he would end up spending the summer and where his friendship with Oil Can would begin. "I fit right in. I had a good spring training, and I made the team as a starting second baseman," he says.

What followed was his best year ever in baseball. He hit .292, fielded superbly, and was named to the Florida State League all-star team. His only disappointment came when, with a month left in the season, he caught his foot in a hole in the basepath and tore a ligament in his knee. The injury ended his season, prevented him from running for five months, and forced him to spend the winter building his strength back up.

This season, too, has been marred by a couple of injuries, which have kept him out of nearly thirty games. First, he twisted an ankle in spring training, and then he experienced a more severe sprain in June. He says, "It's been kind of a rough year, but my manager said to me, 'Maybe it's a good thing that you're getting hurt in the minor leagues, because somewhere along the line you're going to have some good luck ahead of you.' " Still, when he hurt the ankle for the second time, Hundhammer was on a hot streak. Not only was his batting average over .300, he was hitting with power and stealing bases as well.

When he returned to the lineup, it was at third base—a position he had never played in pro ball. Red Sox officials told Hundhammer that, with Jerry Remy established at second base in Boston and second baseman Marty Barrett hitting over .300 at the Class AAA team in Pawtucket, Rhode Island, he might have a better chance to move up at third base than at second. It might also be that the Red Sox believe that Hundhammer's best hope of making the majors is not as an everyday player but as a utility man—someone who can fill in at several positions. "What it does is open up some opportunities for me," he said, when first moved to third.

Playing third, however, required him to learn a new position under game conditions. "The positions are completely different," he says. "They demand different types of throwing, different types of fielding. It's a completely different game mentally because of the plays you're making."

Hundhammer struggled. He made half a dozen errors during his first two weeks at third, and while his fielding improved after that, his batting average began to slide as he labored to adapt to the new position.

One evening, while still playing third, he explained, "It's hurt my hitting a little bit because I've concentrated so much on my defense. Right now I'm just trying to pick up on my hitting again, and hopefully with my hitting the rest of my game will fall into place. I think, overall, I'm doing a pretty fair job at third—for a beginner. It's really not easy to be a beginner in Double A. I mean, it's not like starting in high school where no one really cares how you're doing. This is my job, and it means a lot to me, and all of a sudden I'm playing someplace I never played before."

When Hundhammer made two errors in the first game of a doubleheader in mid-August, Torchia, the manager, abruptly ended the experiment. Back at second, Hundhammer had a couple of weeks left in the season to try to boost his batting average and repair the damage that had been done to his confidence.

This evening's game proceeds uneventfully through the middle innings. The Bristol hitters, sitting on their 4–0 lead, show no more punch as Reading's Smith sets them down in order through the fourth, fifth, and sixth innings. Hundhammer gets his third turn at the plate in the bottom of the sixth and grounds out to short.

Boyd, meanwhile, has allowed a couple of singles but nothing more. In the top of the seventh, Hundhammer gets his first chance in the field, handling a routine grounder with ease. When the next batter taps a soft roller up the middle, Hundhammer scrambles to his right, grabs the ball with his bare hand, and shovels it to first in time for the out. It is a nifty play, and Boyd, watching it, jerks his right arm up in the air to give the out sign and grins back at Hundhammer. After Boyd strikes out the next batter, he gets a pat on the rear from Hundhammer, and they trot off the diamond together.

Such expressions of team spirit and camaraderie can be seen on baseball teams at every level, but players—even those who have been in the majors for some time—say their closest friendships were formed in the minor leagues. Without such friendships, being a minor leaguer would be a very lonely experience. Both Boyd and Hundhammer are so far from home that their families have never seen them play professional baseball, and both have girlfriends who are far away.

Nevertheless, both have adjusted fairly well to their new lives. "I pretty much want to be alone when I'm playing ball," Boyd says. "It doesn't really excite me for my parents to come to the ballgame, because they've seen me play all my life. They get the *Sporting News*, and as long as they see I'm in the top stats, that's all they need to know."

Hundhammer seems a bit lonelier. He is looking forward to the end of the season and the chance to go home to California and see his girlfriend, Linda. They plan to marry in the fall.

"I really miss her, because I do enjoy going out for a nice dinner or going to a show. I want to be married and be with my wife, and in a nice place with our furniture and in a big bed and enjoying life. That's how I am. I like the finer things in life," he says.

"But," he goes on, "I know I've got a job to do, and I know I've got better times ahead of me . . . so I'm willing to wait. Actually, it's not that bad. I love what I'm doing, so as long as I keep my mind on the playing field, I don't get down about it."

Both players live in Bristol. Hundhammer has been given a room, rent-free, in the house of a seventy-six-year-old fan who enjoys the company of the young players. Boyd rents a small apartment, which he shares with a teammate. They each earn about $1,500 a month.

Since the Red Sox play nearly all their games at night, the players have their mornings and early afternoons free. Hundhammer spends his free time reading the papers, doing errands, and occasionally playing a round of golf. "Pretty much I'm just kind of waiting around for the afternoon, when I go to the ballpark," he says. "There really isn't much to do. Your mind—most of the guys that do well—your mind is on baseball. There's so much to learn about this game."

Boyd, too, sees his off-the-field activities pretty much as a matter of killing time. He sometimes joins a group of players for an afternoon at a mall or for a few beers at a disco at night, but he also spends time alone. "I find myself doing that a lot—just being by myself and concentrating on my baseball. There's not much else to do," he says. "It's good for you because you're a different crop of guys and you're pretty much . . . you're blessed. You're in your own little world of baseball."

That sense of inhabiting a world of their own binds the players together. Since they hope to move on next season to a higher level of the game in another town, the players say there is little reason to build close relationships with the townspeople in Bristol. They socialize among themselves, sharing the risks and possibilities of their lives as young ballplayers.

"It's pretty much of a family, not just this team, just the whole league in general, just baseball in general," Boyd says. "It really brings guys together, and you have a friend for a long time. He might get released, but you could call that guy up in the off-season and you always got a friend."

Boyd and Hundhammer have grown close since they met last

summer in Winter Haven. They were first drawn together, in part, by their differences: neither Boyd, the cocksure black kid from Mississippi, nor Hundhammer, the quieter and more sophisticated Californian, had ever come across anyone like the other before.

"Dennis is a character," Hundhammer says. "He's from the deep South, he's from a completely different economic background, he's really just so different from anybody else. But he's got a lot of desire to be a big league player and I do, too. I think that's our common ground."

Hundy obviously enjoys talking about his friend. "He just interests me as an individual," he goes on. "He's not normal. He's cocky. He doesn't mind telling you that he's great, which is not like me at all. I consider myself to be not as cocky as Oil. But I respect him because he wants to be a big league player, and he thinks he is one. We like to talk baseball. I think he understands the game better and better each day, and I just learn from him."

Together, Boyd and Hundhammer are immersed in baseball. While Boyd brings more emotion to the game, Hundhammer is a student of baseball, always searching for the ingredients of success. "If I ever make it to the big leagues," he says, "the first guy I go talk to is Carl Yazstremski. I want to know what made him become a big leaguer for twenty years, what kind of dedication, what kind of work, what did it for him."

For now, Oil Can and Hundy spend hours each week talking about the game—during warm-ups, on the bench, in the eight- and ten-hour bus rides to away games, in hotel rooms late at night. They are faithful readers of the sports pages and the *Sporting News*, charting the progress of their friends and rivals. Baseball is serious business to them.

Still, humor—usually supplied by Oil Can—also plays an important part in their friendship. The humor is of the usual locker room variety: boasts, put-downs, and taunts, all meant in good fun.

Recalling his first encounters with Hundy, Oil Can says, "I would always be on the bench, and I was always sarcastic, and first he thought I was just a hot dog and I ran my mouth a lot. Then he got to know me a little bit and he said, well, this guy's just crazy and he's a lot of fun. My sense of humor just rubbed off on him."

Oil Can starts laughing, just from thinking about their kidding around. "Sometimes I come to the clubhouse, and I get all over him. I tease him about he's white, and he teases me about I'm black, and we just go all down with it. But it turns out to be we're real close and off-season he might have written me twenty times. I got letters, always inspirational things, always telling me he wants me to do good.

"And when he plays behind me, I can hear him when I can't hear nobody."

Going into the top of the eighth, Boyd has allowed just three hits. He gives up a couple more singles in that inning, allowing Reading two baserunners in one inning for the first time in the game. But he ends the threat by inducing the dangerous Fryer to bounce out to short.

Hundhammer is the fourth man due up in Bristol's eighth, but the side goes down in order and he gets no farther than the on-deck circle, where a teenage girl persuades him to turn for a quick snapshot. He is 0 for 3 on the night, and his average has dipped two points to .268.

In the ninth, Boyd retires the first hitter on a fly ball and strikes out the second. Then Ray Borucki, Reading's second baseman, hits a slow grounder to Whittemore at first who flips the ball over to Boyd. Trying to snap it smartly into his glove, Boyd misplays the ball. "I wanted to go out in style," he says afterward. "I wanted to get it so bad that I slapped at it."

The miscue makes no difference. Boyd strikes out the next man, Nemeth, for the third time in the game, and thus ends one of his finest pitching performances of the season. He demonstrated his control by throwing 116 pitches, 86 of them for strikes. He struck out 11 and didn't walk anybody. He permitted just 5 hits, and didn't allow an opposing batter past second base. He accepts congratulations from his teammates as he leaves the mound and, just as he reaches the dugout, happily flips the ball into the stands.

By now the night has grown chilly, and this summer of baseball in Bristol is almost over. The Red Sox sweep the series against Reading, though Hundhammer—his frustration rising to the surface—is thrown out of the next night's game in the first inning for arguing a called third strike. He manages to hit well in the remaining games, raising his average to .272, and goes home for the winter to California.

His thoughts are first on his upcoming marriage and then on next spring, when the Red Sox will decide whether to keep him for another year in Bristol or move him up to their top farm club in Pawtucket. He has just turned twenty-four.

"Right now, I would definitely come back and play in Double A next year," Hundhammer says. "If things didn't work out, I would have to take a serious look at it—at how I'm playing and if I'm getting better or if I'm not, and what the plans are with the club.

"This is not a game where you can just set a timetable for yourself and say, I want to be in A ball, then Double A, then

Triple A, then the big leagues. It just doesn't happen that way. There are just too many other good ballplayers."

He mentions that so many of the things that affect a player's career are beyond his control: injuries, trades, the competition and caliber of players already in the organization. He may be thinking that Remy, the Red Sox second baseman, could be around for a long time.

Nor can Hundhammer shop around for a different team, where his chances might be better. He is contractually bound to the Red Sox, and they will decide how far and how fast he may travel on the long road to the big leagues. "It's so easy to talk about that now, how you cannot control things," he says. "But when you actually sit down and think about yourself, you wish you could control it and say, yeah, I'd like to be in Triple A next year. I would like to be in Triple A very much next year. But I'm being realistic. I imagine I'll be here. I won't be disappointed if I'm here. I just hope I get better."

Boyd pitches once more, in the last game of the season at Lynn. While he is warming up before the game, Torchia gives him some exciting news: Boston wants him to join the major league club for the last month of the season. Boyd loses a heartbreaker to Lynn, 2–1, and two weeks later he takes the mound at Fenway Park for the opening game of a doubleheader against the Cleveland Indians.

Boyd pitches effectively, scattering seven hits and allowing two runs in 5⅓ innings, but he and the Red Sox lose the game, 3–1. He says afterward, "I feel I did alright for my first time out. But it wasn't nothing like I can throw the ball."

Boyd, nevertheless, is fortunate. He is just where he wants to be, and he is confident that he will have a good chance to make the Red Sox next spring.

"I would like to be around baseball all my life," he says. "I want to be a manager some day. I really do. I want to be manager of a high school baseball team.

"Somebody's going to recognize that I have a good baseball mind when I get older. I'll be a baseball fanatic when I get older. I know I will. I'll just be wild about it."

# 3 On the Verge: *Ron Darling of the Tidewater Tides*

He is friendly and charming and as handsome as a movie star, a college man from Yale. He stands 6 feet 3 inches tall and weighs 200 pounds. His shoulders are broad, his waist is narrow, his legs are long and powerful. His fastball, clocked at better than 90 miles an hour, is overpowering, and his slider is even better.

He seems, in short, to possess the stuff that baseball stardom is made of. Even his name: Ron Darling. With a name like that, how can he possibly miss?

Ron Darling has just turned twenty-two during this summer of 1982, but already great things are expected of him. Once a pitching sensation for Yale, Darling is now on the verge of becoming a major leaguer with the New York Mets. He is thought by some to be the young pitcher the Mets need to become winners again, perhaps the best young prospect the team has had since Tom Seaver.

If Ron Darling seems too good to be true, just listen to what people are saying about him.

Listen, for example, to Lou Gorman, the vice president of

the Mets, who is responsible for developing his team's young talent. Gorman resisted the temptation to make Darling a big leaguer in 1982—a bad year for the Mets and a good one for Darling, who pitched for the Tidewater Tides, New York's Class AAA farm team in Norfolk, Virginia.

"The temptation is to bring him up right away," Gorman said that summer. "He's as polished a pitcher as you'll ever see. He's poised, intelligent, composed—he's got a live arm with an above-average major league fastball, a good curve and slider, and a good change of speed. He's a solid front-liner but we don't want to push it. The ability and potential is there but we're going to bite the bullet and hang on."*

Or listen to Ken MacKenzie, a pitcher for the original Mets of 1962 and later the baseball coach who helped recruit Darling

---

* *New York Daily News,* July 11, 1982.

for Yale. Darling went on to break half a dozen college records —for hitting as well as for pitching.

"He had the greatest year a pitcher's ever had at Yale. Just Frank Merriwell all over," MacKenzie says, referring to a fictional sports hero at Yale. "If you needed a home run to win the game, he'd hit it. He won a couple of games with catches in the outfield. He was just fantastic."

Or listen to Darling himself: "This will probably sound egotistical, but when I'm playing well, I think I can decide any game—my pitching, my hitting, you know, something."*

Like many up-and-coming ballplayers, Darling sounds a little cocky, even boastful, when he evaluates his talents. He compares himself to the great ones. But his confidence seems genuine, not bluster.

"I think I have all the physical abilities to be a great pitcher in the major leagues. It's just mentally getting to the point where you can win every time out," he says. "Guys like Carlton and Tom Seaver and Valenzuela and Pete Vukovich—they're at a point in their career that, when they pitch, they're just confident that they're going to win. I think I'd like to get to the point where they are."

Getting to that point, of course, is the goal of hundreds of very good young pitchers in baseball's minor leagues. Some will succeed but most will not, and predicting major league stardom on the basis of minor league performance is a risky business indeed. In the flood of superlatives that seems to follow Darling wherever he goes, it is easy to lose sight of such facts as this: Ron Darling has yet to pitch a full season in the major leagues.

* *Sports Illustrated*, March 30, 1981.

Signed fresh out of Yale in June 1981, Darling pitched well in his first professional season with the Tulsa Drillers in the Class AA Texas League. But this season, his second as a pro, has brought both good times and bad. He is struggling to keep his record above .500 at Tidewater.

So, even if Darling and his fastball, poured chest-high past frustrated hitters, is a little reminiscent of Tom Seaver, pause for a moment to consider instead the pitching career of Tim Leary. Back in 1980, the hard-throwing Leary drew rave notices in the minors that fed the hopes of long-suffering Met fans. Leary pitched briefly the next spring in New York, but his young arm failed him, and he has been trying to recover ever since.

Think, too, of Frank Quinn. Probably Yale's greatest pitcher before Darling, Quinn was deemed a sure bet for stardom as a prospect with the Boston Red Sox in the 1940s. His big league record can be summed up briefly: nine games in two years, no wins, no losses. He, too, suffered arm trouble.

For the moment, Darling's right arm is strong and sound. But the mortality rate for pitching arms is notoriously high, and the minor league record books are filled with the exploits of young stars who fizzled once they reached the majors. Which is why Ken MacKenzie, for all his enthusiasm about Darling, furrows his brow when he is asked about the young man's prospects. MacKenzie knows that even those players who reach the major leagues cannot count on enjoying a long and successful baseball career. "Going by the percentages, he probably has a 50–50 chance of making it his career," the ex-big leaguer says.

What worries MacKenzie is that Darling does not seem to realize this. After signing his first contract for a hefty bonus, Darling stopped working on his college degree—a degree he will need if his baseball career turns sour. He told one reporter that he would continue his studies under "Professor Seaver."

"That's why I worry a little about Ron Darling," his former coach says. "Why he doesn't have his ass right here."

Ron Darling has decided not to go back to Yale. He has grown accustomed to sunshine, and the sun doesn't shine much during the school year in New Haven. "I don't want to see any more winters," he says.

It is a warm and breezy afternoon in late August 1982 in Norfolk, Virginia, and Darling is enjoying life. He relaxes on the sidelines at Met Park, home of the Tidewater Tides, sweating just a little from a light workout of stretching, running, then throwing. He pitched three days earlier and lost, and isn't scheduled to pitch again for two days, so he has nothing to worry about this afternoon. He has a deep, dark tan, and his eyes light up a little as he talks.

"Probably right here is the best place I could be," he says. "And that's how my life's been. I've been very, very lucky. I didn't have to go up through Rookie or A ball, where the players live in dormitory rooms or live in people's houses or things like that."

For a minor leaguer, Darling is living well and he knows it. He has money in the bank, saved from the $165,000 bonus he was paid for signing a professional contract. His apartment in the nearby resort city of Virginia Beach is a few steps from the ocean. He drives a sports car and is doing some television work for a local station when he has the time. "I'm having a good time," he says. "I feel like a kid."

Not that it's all been easy. Getting minor league hitters out has been tougher than pitching to collegians, and Darling has had a few nights on the mound that he'd like to forget. Traveling to away games—especially last season with Tulsa—sometimes meant long and dusty overnight bus trips lasting ten or twelve hours.

"I'm sure people who have been on ten-hour bus trips would read that and say ballplayers are just babies or whatever, but you take a ten-hour bus trip after you've played a game for three hours and then have to play the next day, and do that consistently for a whole year, and I don't think anyone would say that again," he says.

Those days, however, are now behind him. While it is still a half-day trip from Norfolk to, say, Rochester, New York, the Tides travel by plane. The schedule includes more off-days. And Norfolk's Met Park is everything the home of a Class AAA team should be: clean and spacious, well-lit and well-maintained. It has more of a major league feeling than most backwater parks—lots of foul territory separates the playing field from the fans, some of whom watch games from a stadium dining room where they can order dinner.

Still, Darling has no intention of staying long. "It's just against your nature to settle into a place where you don't really want to be. You're here and this is just a stopover," he says.

Darling expects that his next stop will be Shea Stadium in New York. But his arrival time is by no means certain, since he is just one of several promising young pitchers with the 1982 Tides. Brent Gaff, the ace of the staff, already had a chance with the Mets but flopped, getting hit hard and losing several games in a row. He is now back in Tidewater. Scott Holman also made the trip to New York and back.

Darling knows that he will have to wait his turn, at least until spring 1983 and possibly longer. "I think I still need to be here in Tidewater," he says. "I have enough good stuff that I could probably win in the majors here and there. But when I do go up, I want to be able to win consistently."

On a Christmas morning in 1965, five-year-old Ron Darling found a small plastic fielder's glove under the family tree. "I wanted to go out and play right away," he recalls. "But there was two feet of snow on the ground. So my dad and I threw a tennis ball around the house."*

Like so many professional athletes, Darling comes from an athletic family. His father, Ron Sr., grew up in Vermont, where in high school he made the all-state teams in baseball and football. He turned down a couple of college scholarships, opting instead for an Air Force career. In the late 1950s, he was sent to Hawaii, where he married Luciana Mikina Aikala, a Hawaiian-Chinese woman. Their first child, Ron Jr., was born on August 19, 1960.

"The first time I ever started playing baseball was with my father," Ron says. "When I was five years old, he used to hit me a hundred ground balls and he used to pitch me a hundred so I could bat. He loved baseball."

By the time the Darlings had moved to Millbury, Massachusetts, a suburb of Worcester, Ron Sr. had determined that his son's life would be different from his own—it would include college as well as sports. "My parents were very academic conscious," Ron says. "That's good for any kid, I think, because there's not that many kids who can play professional sports. It's some minuscule number, so I think they were going with the odds."

---

* *New Haven Register,* March 1, 1981.

He enrolled at St. John's High School, a rigorous parochial school in nearby Shrewsbury, which had a fine sports program. "It was probably one of the best things that could happen to me," he says. '"It is an all-Catholic boys school—suitcoat and tie every day. It was good to have a little bit of discipline." It is characteristic of Darling, who seems mature beyond his years, to see the value of the strict rules that students must live by in parochial schools.

Darling became a classic high school sports hero. In football—his favorite sport at the time—he starred as a quarterback and as a defensive back, winning all-state honors and football scholarship offers from such colleges as Clemson and Stamford. He could dunk a basketball and run the 60-yard dash in 6.4 seconds. As for baseball, he was an outstanding hitter, an every-day player at shortstop, and an occasional late-inning relief pitcher.

Sports came easily to him. Playing in an American Legion baseball league one summer, Darling, a natural right-handed hitter, decided to try switch-hitting. He hit a three-run homer his first time up left-handed and added a double and single by day's end.

His future in sports seemed to be either as a football quarter-back or a baseball shortstop. College recruiters from across the country became frequent visitors to the Darling home.

"He was it. He was Mr. New England," MacKenzie says. "Whatever we could do, we would roll out the red carpet. There was no question that he could be a college star."

Darling selected Yale because of the school's emphasis on academics. He did not want to attend a so-called jock factory. "I kind of played the odds myself," he says. "I wanted something to back me up in case I did not make it in sports."

His career as a pitcher began to take shape because of two things that happened—one an accident, the second more deliberate—during his freshman year. First, playing freshman football, Darling suffered a series of head injuries. He had blacked out a couple of times in high school, too, and doctors now warned him that the structure of his head left him vulnerable to concussions.

"I thought I'd better give up the sport before it made me quit sports forever," he says. "I decided to concentrate on baseball."

Joe Benanto, Yale's baseball coach, couldn't have asked for better news. No Yale team had managed a winning season in 10 years, so the college's baseball program badly needed a spark.

"Ronnie was important because he changed us almost overnight," Benanto says. "You could tell he was going to be great, right off the bat—just the way he carried himself, the way he threw the ball. Everything he did, he did big league as a freshman. He just gave you that impression. He was head and shoulders above everybody else."

But Benanto also persuaded Darling to give up shortstop—his hands were a little "hard," in baseball parlance, for the position—and work harder on his pitching. Darling was such a good hitter that he continued to play every day as an outfielder, and he batted .320. But he also pitched in twenty-one of the team's thirty games, mostly in relief. In the last game of the season, a big game against the University of New Haven, Darling pitched a 4–1 complete game victory by using a new pitch, the slider, with great success.

By his sophomore year, Darling was nearly unstoppable as he focused more on pitching. "My coach told me to concentrate on pitching, because I could make some money in the game if I did," he remembers.

Behind Darling, Yale rolled to its best baseball record in thirty years. He started twelve games, finished all twelve, and chalked up an 11–2 record and a 1.31 ERA. He hit, too, for a school record .384 batting average and a .589 slugging percentage.

That summer, Darling had a chance to show off both his batting and pitching power in an amateur all-star game at Yankee Stadium. First, he hit a 450-foot home run and two doubles. Then, he was called in to pitch with a one-run lead and the winning runs on base in the ninth. He struck out two men and retired the third on a popup. Says Benanto, "It was like a storybook."

Darling played with an intensity that was sometimes surprising. Some pro scouts suggested that he concentrate on pitching, but he wanted to play—and play hard—every day.

When Yale's team took its annual southern trip to begin the season in the spring of his junior year, Darling performed before a crowd of scouts and major league players at the Lakeland, Florida, spring training base of the Detroit Tigers. Benanto remembers that Darling pitched well and then doubled late in the game to knock in the go-ahead runs for Yale.

"He got to third base with one out, and there was a ground ball hit to the infield. He came flying home, and he dove head first into the catcher," Benanto says. "The goddamned scouts, I thought they were going to have a nervous breakdown.

"So I said, 'Ronnie, what the hell are you doing? You have to hook slide into the plate so you don't get hurt.' He said, 'But coach—he was blocking the plate. I had to get him out of the way.' That's the way he was. He was such a competitor that the future was not as important to him as winning."

Darling's last game as a college pitcher was his best. On May 22, 1981, he faced St. John's in an NCAA Regional Tournament game in New Haven that will always be remembered by the 2,500 fans who were lucky enough to be there.

Darling and his mound opponent that day, Frank Viola, were considered the best college pitchers in the Northeast, and both lived up to expectations. Through the first nine innings and then the tension-packed tenth and eleventh, Viola used a baffling assortment of sliders and sinkers to shut out the Yale batsmen.

Darling was even better. He pitched no-hit ball through those 11 innings, firing his rising, letter-high fastballs past the hitters and then fooling them with what had become his most dangerous and effective pitch—a wicked, sharp-breaking slider thrown down around the knees. (The slider reminded some fans of the one thrown so effectively by Ron Guidry of the New York Yankees.)

Darling, of course, remembers the game vividly. "It was just one of those things where I had the best stuff I've ever had. Everything worked well. Everything. Even if I made a mistake, they'd miss it or something," he says. "I was more intense than I've ever been, but I was still enjoying myself. I could feel everything that was going on."

Benanto calls it the greatest exhibition of pitching he's ever seen. "He was incredible. They just couldn't touch the ball," he says. "It was like a man toying with little boys."

In the twelfth inning, Steve Scafa, St. John's pesky second baseman, led off with the team's first hit—a liner off the handle of the bat into left field. The spectators, the players from both teams, and even some of the scouts rose to honor Darling with an ovation.

When the game resumed, Scafa quickly stole second and third. St. John's put another runner on after an error by the shortstop, but with two men out, Darling was working on the hitter and still hoping to get out of the jam. He didn't. St. John's tried a double steal, Yale's catcher tried to throw out the runner at second, and the runner got caught in a rundown long enough for Scafa to tear home. Yale couldn't score in the bottom of the inning, and the game was over.

Darling, normally poised, first stammers just a little when he talks about the game, then ducks the question: how did it feel to lose despite pitching so well? "It's hard for me to explain, because not only was it a fine pitching performance, the best pitching performance I've had, but also it was at a school where baseball isn't that big, where 2,500 people were standing up the whole game from about the ninth inning on, where people were going crazy and yelling and scouts were jumping on their feet. It was just one of those games that, I guess, happens just once in a lifetime to most people. But hopefully it won't be the last time for me."

Darling then let it be known that he was willing to turn professional that summer for the right money. The Seattle Mariners, who had the first pick in the annual draft of college and high school players, seriously considered making him the top choice in the country. They were impressed by his personality as well as by his athletic ability.

"He has character, poise, and he's obviously well-disciplined," said Bill Kearns, a top scout for the Mariners. "He's the kind of kid who'll never miss a team bus or get involved in so many of those minor irritations that we seem to have today. We know that he's a solid citizen."*

Other teams voiced similar sentiments. It was an exciting

---

* *New Haven Journal Courier,* May 22, 1981.

time for Darling. "The scouts called me and talked to me and were telling me that I was either one or two on their lists," he says.

But the Mariners were apparently put off by Darling's demand for a signing bonus of about $150,000 (they didn't want to pay more than $75,000) and by his decision to hire an agent to help him get it. Instead, they chose Mike Moore, a highly regarded pitcher from Oral Roberts University in Oklahoma. (Later, given a chance in the big leagues, Moore proved anew that there is no such thing as a "can't miss" player when he was ineffective and was sent back to the minors.)

Darling became the ninth player drafted when the Texas Rangers picked him in the first round. Since so many people expected him to be the first or second player chosen, being picked ninth was a little disappointing. But being a first round choice was still an honor, and Darling wasn't complaining.

"Texas," he said with a smile after hearing the news. "Everyone knows there are more millionaires in Texas than anywhere else." Darling got his $165,000—not bad for a twenty-year-old college junior.*

He was happy with the bonus, but some other minor leaguers, working for $1,500 or $2,000 a month, were understandably jealous. When Darling arrived in Tulsa, Oklahoma, the home of the Rangers' Tulsa Drillers farm team in the Class AA Texas League, the name on his locker was written "$Darling." His first bus trip with the team was long and lonely.

But Darling slowly won the respect of his teammates by showing he could pitch. He started strong, winning two games without a loss and striking out 29 men in his first 29⅓ innings.

Then, for the first time, some of the glow surrounding his

---

* *Worcester Evening Gazette,* June 9, 1981.

career began to wear off. He was bombed in a couple of games, and coaches began to worry about a flaw in his pitching delivery —a hesitation and a tendency not to bend over quite far enough —that scouts had noticed in college.

"I had a real bad spell," he says ruefully. "I had mononucleosis. My arm was getting dead. It lasted for five starts. In pro ball, you have to be at your best every night. It was sort of a rude awakening. I needed that."

The slump ended as suddenly as it had begun. Darling's last three starts for Tulsa were all two-hitters, two of them shutouts and the last a 1–0 loss in the league playoffs. Reflecting on the transition from college to the pros, he now says, "It was a lot less difficult than I thought."

There was even talk the next spring that he would be given a shot in the majors with Texas. Yet after working out some with the Rangers in spring training in Pompano Beach, Darling was preparing to report to Denver, Texas' club in the Class AAA American Association.

Then came April Fools Day. "I went out for dinner, and I came home at about ten o'clock and there were three phone messages. I was supposed to call Joe Klein, the farm director of the Rangers, Eddie Robinson, the general manager of the Rangers, and Lou Gorman, the farm director of the Mets," Darling says. He couldn't reach Klein or Robinson. "So I called Lou Gorman, and he told me, 'Congratulations, you're now with the Mets.' " It was no prank.

Darling was shocked—it's unusual for a team to part with its top draft pick—and so were some fans in New York. The Mets had given up a box office favorite, center fielder Lee Mazzilli, to get two pitchers, Darling and Walt Terrell, who had worked the previous season in the Texas League.

Once Darling thought about the trade, though, he was

pleased. "If I ever do well in New York, the outside monies you can make are tremendous," he says. "My parents can come and watch the games. And the opportunity to play with the Mets is great because their pitching isn't that strong." He drove across south Florida to the Mets' base in St. Petersburg, and was assigned to Tidewater, the team's top farm club in the International League.

Darling was right on schedule. When he signed a pro contract, he said he wanted to pitch in the majors within two years. Now he was just a step away.

"The biggest jump in baseball is from Double A to Triple A," he says. "Double A is mostly a place where players are on their way up. Triple A is a place where players are just about ready, and players have come down because they just weren't ready enough. You've got players who are just on the verge of being major league players every day."

Now Darling was in a league with players whose names are familiar to many fans. Mike Cubbage, who played the infield for several years with the Minnesota Twins, played first for Tidewater. Butch Hobson, who used to be the regular third baseman for the Boston Red Sox, played for the Columbus Clippers. And Darling's mound opponents that summer included such onetime major leaguers as Mark Fidrych and Dave Ford.

As the season began, Darling pitched superbly. He allowed only one run in each of his first two outings, though he came away with no decision in the first game and lost the second, 1–0, on a ninth-inning home run.

"I lost a lot of close ones, so many in school or college that it's weird," he says. "But sooner or later in a zero–zero game, I won't be the one making the mistakes."

Though his record didn't show it right away, Darling was

proving that he could get hitters out at the Class AAA level. Soon the victories came. He was at his best in June, throwing two shutouts and a 4–1 complete game win that improved his season record to 6–3. At that point, Darling led the league in earned run average with a 2.39 mark, and he had struck out 71 batters in 83 innings. He began to attract notices in the newspapers in New York.

His winning streak ended when Darling left a game early with a bruised ankle, and in his next outing he was hit hard. A couple of hard-luck losses—by 2–1 and 2–0 scores to the Richmond Braves—followed before his real troubles began.

On July 22, the headline in the local paper, the *Norfolk Virginian Pilot,* read: "Tides Fall to Syracuse, Darling Hurt." Darling had pitched eight strong innings in another losing effort, but, much more ominously, he had left the ballgame with a muscle spasm in his right forearm.

"I had a twinge after I broke off a curve ball in the seventh and then another in the eighth," he told a reporter after the game. "I don't think it's anything to be alarmed about. It wasn't a pop or anything like that."

Still, there was reason for concern. Throwing fastballs at speeds of better than 90 miles an hour inevitably strains the arm and shoulder muscles. Throwing breaking balls with a snapping motion generates even greater stresses. It has become routine for pitchers to submerge their throbbing arms in ice after each game, and the threat of a sore arm, which can be a career-ending problem, hangs over every pitcher.

Until the game at Syracuse, Darling's arm seemed immune to the everyday troubles of most hurlers. Perhaps because his pitching career began so late, he does not soak his arm in ice after throwing and has never experienced serious arm trouble.

In fact, Darling took the mound again just four days later at Rochester. But he left the game in the first inning after walking three men, allowing a single, and retiring only two batters. "I just got behind the batters and started pressing," he said, insisting that his arm felt fine.*

The last six weeks of the season were not happy ones. On occasion, Darling pitched well, but more often he was ineffective. He had problems with his control, walking five men in each of two games and seven in another. Jack Aker, his manager, detected some of the same flaws in his delivery that coaches had noted earlier; he was rocking back too far in an effort to get something extra on the ball.

Those who watched Darling at the time think that, feeling a great deal of pressure to perform well, he began overthrowing and trying to do more than he was capable of doing. That only compounded his problems and caused him more worry. "Self-doubt is the worst thing," he says. "Batters who are in slumps have self-doubt. Pitchers who aren't pitching well have self-doubt."

The low point came in mid-August against the Columbus Clippers, a team packed with powerful hitters. Darling suffered through 4⅓ innings, allowing 9 hits, walking 5, and giving up 12 runs in a humiliating 20–1 defeat.

His last outing of the season was also against Columbus. He gave up two more home runs to Steve Balboni, a slugging first baseman, and left in the fourth inning. Much to his dismay, he was not called upon again by Aker as Tidewater swept through two rounds of league playoffs.

After starting so strongly, Darling ended the season with a

---

* *The Norfolk Virginian Pilot,* July 26, 1982.

7–9 record and a 3.73 ERA–his first losing record ever in baseball. The statistics, of course, tell only part of the story. If his teammates had scored a few more runs in the games when he pitched well, Darling could have finished with ten or eleven victories. ("I've lost two 1–0 games, two 2–0 games, a 2–1 game, and I've left many games zero to zero," he notes.) But his late season difficulties, which are of much greater concern than his record, cannot be attributed to bad luck.

Explanations for his troubles are not hard to find. While Darling maintains that his sporadic arm problems weren't serious, he admits that his arm tired by the end of the season. Neither pitching for Yale nor his half-season at Tulsa fully prepared him for the rigors of the long summer at Tidewater.

"This is the first time I've thrown this many innings, and I'm a little tired," he says. "When my arm was sound, I've pitched against these hitters as good as anyone's ever pitched against them."

The Mets' high expectations for Darling, who was only twenty-one when the season began, probably put extra pressure on him. While Darling was pitching well in June and July, reporters from New York newspapers made the trip to Virginia to speculate about whether he was ready for the Mets.

Benanto, his Yale coach, asks, "How many pitchers do you know in the minor leagues who have had to pitch with the pressure that that kid's had on him? I've seen articles in every newspaper in the country. It is a lot of pressure on a kid."

Darling's early season success—in fact, the remarkable success he had enjoyed at every level of the game—made it that much harder for him to adjust to the hard times that followed. In retrospect, it seems that the more he tried to correct his mechanical problems or compensate for his minor injuries, the worse things got. He now calls the season a "character builder."

"It's just sort of mellowed me about the game. It used to be, just go out and be so intense and just throw hard and get people out. Here, you've got to be a little more mellow, because you've got so many more starts and you pitch so many more innings and you have so many more rough jams that you have to take everything with a grain of salt," he says.

"I try now not to get too high up over my victories and not to get too low in my defeats. If I win, that's great. But if I lose, that's going to happen, too, so just wait for the next game and do better the next time out," Darling concludes. Peculiar as it sounds, the season taught him something he had never needed to know before: how to deal with defeat.

Perhaps Darling, as a collegian, was already blessed with what the scouts like to call a "major league arm." He certainly possessed the intelligence and the intensity that contribute to success in sports. What he lacked, however, was seasoning—the experience that comes only from pitching in dozens of games, to hundreds of batters, in countless different situations. That experience, which simply cannot be taught, is probably the most valuable thing Darling got from his season.

The next spring, Darling was invited to spring training with the Mets. The thrill didn't last long. He pitched only one inning in an exhibition game, giving up four runs to the Toronto Blue Jays, before returning to Tidewater.

The tryout with the Mets, however, taught him something. "Being around big league pitchers, I recognized that it's not their physical gifts that keep them in the big leagues but their mental gifts—their poise and understanding of the game," he said.*

---

* *New York Post,* March 25, 1983.

Toiling for Tidewater in 1983, Darling had fallen behind his own schedule. He had hoped to spend just two years in the minors and this was his third. Still, he was just twenty-two and had only been pitching for four years. Some of his teammates had pitched since their Little League days.

His second summer in Tidewater was more successful. He improved his won-lost mark to 10–9, taking six of his last seven starts. While he used to try to impress his manager and coaches by striking batters out, Darling now focused less on throwing hard and more on changing speeds and on control. He tried to keep the ball down when possible. His arm problems of the previous summer did not resurface, and late in the season, Darling was called up to New York, where new tests awaited him.

He hoped never to return to Tidewater, but even as he joined the Mets, Darling realized that the two summers he had spent with the Tides had been critical to his development as a pitcher. In Tidewater, he left the charmed world of college and the low minor leagues behind and began to mature into a major leaguer.

By the end of his second summer, Darling had learned how to pace himself, physically and mentally, through the rigors of a long season. He was forced to cope with injuries and overcame them. He found himself in pressure situations—pitching from behind in the count to experienced batters, pitching in the late innings of close games, pitching after being hit hard in his previous outing. He figured out how to make the best use of his repertoire of pitches and developed his ability to think on the mound. He began to discover his limits.

Slowly, Darling gained confidence in himself and in his ability to pitch in the major leagues. Except for raw talent, confidence is perhaps the most sought-after quality in sports, and certainly one of the most difficult to develop. "You can't last in any sport without being confident," Darling says. "Even if you're not the best, you've got to be confident that you're better than the other guy.

"Especially pitching," he continues. "Ninety percent of it is mental. There's enough guys here who can throw breaking pitches over and have the physical ability, but whether you believe you can do it or whether you believe that you're better than that hitter, I think that's the most important thing.

"This game is a game played with confidence because this game is played with your head. Most people have the physical ability to play this game. To excel in it, I think it's in your head."

# 4 Rookie: *Ron Kittle of the Chicago White Sox*

He is only a rookie, but Ron Kittle has the look of a big leaguer as he walks confidently, menacingly, up to the batter's box to take his stance. He spreads his feet wide and crowds the plate with his 6 feet 4 inch, 210 pound frame. Then he takes a few practice swings, and the bat comes around so hard on the last one that his right hand lets go on the follow through. Whoosh! It's enough to give a pitcher the chills.

It's also enough to send shivers of anticipation up a baseball fan's spine. Few things excite fans more than watching a promising young rookie on their favorite team try to make it in the big leagues. For Chicago White Sox fans, as the 1983 season begins, that rookie is Kittle.

Rooting for him is pure pleasure. Kittle's trademark is the home run, a guaranteed crowd pleaser, and he has the ability to hit the long ball as far as anyone in the majors. He is also a local boy, having grown up and gone to school in nearby Gary, Indiana, a gritty factory town where his father is an unemployed steel worker. But his friends and family say fame hasn't changed him a bit, and, in fact, he is an open, friendly, aw-shucks, gee-thanks kind of kid—a pleasing reminder that not all pro athletes are prima donnas with huge salaries and egos to match.

On Opening Day, Kittle isn't in the lineup for the Sox. Yet the twenty-five-year-old rookie enjoys every minute of it. "The whole experience is a real rush," he says. "Opening Day blew me away. Just standing out there when they introduced the starting lineup. . . . Carlton Fisk was on one side of me and Greg Luzinski on the other. . . . What a blast."

He is given a chance to start the game the next day and again the day after that, and the home runs begin to fly. Soon the sight of Kittle striding toward home plate and settling comfortably into his stance becomes a familiar one in Comiskey Park. Some loyal fans can already close their eyes and visualize the tall, lean rookie standing at the plate, waving his long bat.

Yet there is more to Kittle's stance than even the most observant fan can see. For no matter how impressive his physical skills, Ron Kittle's biggest challenge as he begins his rookie year will be to find a mental approach to baseball that will work for him in the big leagues.

He seems to be on the right track there, too. Behind the smiles and the jokes and the easy-going manner that make Ron Kittle so appealing is an unusually determined young man. "I'm not like a lot of self-doubters," he says. "I know I can go out and do the job, and I go out and do it." It's not as easy as that, of course, but determination and self-confidence are as good a place as any to start when trying to define the elements of the right stance. Dozens of rookies, after all, are heralded every spring as the stars of the future, but only a few of them make good right away. For a free-swinging slugger like Kittle, whose big league debut was preceded by an enormous build-up and some impressive statistics, the pressures can be especially intense.

To this point in his career, Kittle has done everything that has been asked of him. He dominated the pitchers at the Class AAA level, smashing 50 home runs, driving in 144 runs, and batting .345 for the Edmonton Trappers, Chicago's top farm team. He has nothing more to prove in the minors.

But skeptics say the minor league parks are bandboxes, hitters' paradises, and that the numbers don't mean a thing. They have examples to prove it, too, from the same Pacific Coast League where Kittle piled up his eye-popping statistics: minor league sensations like Steve Bilko and Bill McNulty who slugged 50 or more homers in the Coast League only to flop when they reached the big time.

For those same players who delight the fans with a tremendous home run are the ones who often disappoint them with a strikeout—usually the result of a wild, hard swing and a miss, sometimes on a ball well outside of the strike zone. The strikeouts come far more often than the homers—typically at a ratio that is better than 2 to 1. Some fans would swear, too, that the strikeouts come at the most critical times.

But, if the strikeouts frustrate the fans, what must they do to the slugger? What must they do, especially, to the rookie who knows that his every trip to the plate is being carefully watched by not only his own manager and teammates but by opposing coaches and players looking for a weakness?

In the minor leagues and in the opening days of his first season, Kittle's strikeouts come as often as his hits. Before getting even his first home run of the year, Kittle strikes out three times in one game. His power is awesome, but so, it seems, will his slumps be deep and worrisome.

Kittle's ability to cope with such successes and failures will be tested frequently during his rookie season. It will take time —and some horrendous slumps—to see whether the young man has the character to rebound from the low points. But there are signs, even during those first days of the spring, that he has the right makeup.

"For a young guy, it's just amazing," marvels Tony LaRussa, the manager of the White Sox. "Nothing bothers him. He can strike out three times—as he has—and not really be concerned or lose confidence. He can get two home runs—like he has—and you don't see a big difference. I think he's got a great attitude."

Charlie Lau, the batting coach for the Sox and the author of a book on hitting,* thinks Kittle has the attributes that a successful slugger needs: a good swing and a strong mind. "Who can peek in the brain? I don't know," Lau says. "But you get to know him a bit and you see there's a toughness about him."

---

* Lau died in March of 1984.

Kittle himself, while outgoing and willing to talk, is not very good at explaining how he deals with the frustrations that go along with his job. He is rarely analytical and tends to laugh off his bad days, saying things like, "It's an experiment for me every time I go up to the plate." This may, however, be a clue to Kittle's strategy for coping with the peaks and valleys of a slugger's life. He sets goals for himself each year but does not dwell on his flaws or setbacks. Unlike some hitters—say, Mike Schmidt or Pete Rose—Kittle is not the type to launch into a detailed explanation of the mechanics of his swing.

While some players pride themselves on the time they spend studying the nuances of baseball, Kittle takes a simpler approach. He arrives at the ballpark each day with two things in mind: to work as hard as he can and to enjoy himself.

"They say you play like you practice, so I practice hard. I spend a lot of hours at it," Kittle says. "You may not win that day, but if everybody plays hard, you're doing your job.

"I just want to go up there and prove myself," he continues. "People in the stands may question you or they call you a bum and all that stuff, but I just put that out of my mind. I say, 'Hey, I've got my chance and I'm going to take advantage of it.'

"There's a lot of determination in me."

To find the roots of Ronald Dale Kittle's determination, you have to leave Chicago and travel east for about half an hour along I–94 to Gary, Indiana. The Kittles live in the Aetna section, a neighborhood of post-World War II tract housing that has seen better days. If the paint is peeling a bit on some of the houses, be aware that the owners might not have the money to repaint right now. This is a neighborhood that grew up around the steel industry, and it has suffered along with the steel mills that once powered Gary. The city's biggest employer, U.S. Steel, once had 12,000 people on the payroll; now it has only 7,000.

While Ron Kittle is piling up some fine statistics during his rookie season in Chicago, the most-watched number in Gary is the unemployment rate. It hovers at around 12 percent, and Ron's father, James Kittle, an ironworker, is one of the jobless. Ron's high school buddies are also in and out of jobs.

"They get laid off and they get hired back, they get laid off and they get hired back," Kittle says. "It's crazy. They never know what's going to happen, except they're pretty sure it will be bad."*

The Kittles, father and son, decided early on that baseball could help Ron escape the gray world of the mills. James Kittle never played organized ball, but he remembers growing up in West Virginia and walking twelve to fifteen miles every Sunday to play on a sandlot field from morning until dark. It was much easier for young Ron to play ball since the Kittle home in Gary is right across the street from a Little League field. During warm weather, Ron could nearly always be found on the field—if he wasn't playing some other sport somewhere else.

"I wouldn't say I was a nervous kid, but I was always on the go. I played baseball, football, and basketball. I played just about everything there was, tennis, ping pong," Ron recalls. "If it wasn't pertaining to sports, I really didn't care too much about it."

He started playing baseball in Little League. "It was an eight-year-olds' league, and I was seven and a half, and they

---

* *Chicago Sun Times,* March 24, 1983.

snuck me in," he says. "Ever since I saw a few ball games, and I kind of liked it when I was growing up, I always had that dream inside me that one day I was going to be a major league ballplayer."

The six children in the family were all encouraged to participate in sports, and father James, who is long and lean like his son, coached youth baseball teams for seven years. "My dad liked sports," Ron says, "but he never pushed us into anything. He got us the best equipment we could use, and he just really enjoyed it and so did the whole family."

Today James Kittle won't take any of the credit for his son's success. "Determination and hard work," he says firmly. "Ronnie made himself what he is by hard work." Ron "would hit home runs at the park and then go to bed with a bat, why . . . you'd hear the bat roll out of the bed at night and you knew he was thinking baseball," James says.*

As a teenager, Ron played all over the field—first base, catcher, shortstop, and outfield. He was always a natural power hitter, even as a tyke. "Even when I was playing Little League, I was noticed as one of the top ballplayers," he says. "They'd say, 'Hey, there's Ronnie. We want Ronnie on our team.' "

He went to Gary Wirt High School, a small school but one that always produced top sports teams. His high school coach, Jerry Troxel, remembers Kittle as an awesome hitter and a genuine pleasure to coach. Kittle stills visits the school now and then.

The entire Kittle family, in fact, is remembered fondly by Troxel. "Ron would mow the grass at the field, drag it, groom it. He'd do it all himself," Troxel says. "His mom and dad

---

* *Gary Post Tribune,* May 15, 1983.

used to be in the booster club. She used to bake cookies and everything."

Kittle's first taste of the professional baseball scene came when, as a high school sophomore, he went to a couple of the open tryout camps held periodically by big league teams. Scouts use the camps to screen players who may be drafted later.

"I did real well," he remembers. "As a matter of fact, a couple of my friends and I went to one, and we were the top three in the whole camp. In my junior year, we went back and we were still in the top three. Then, in high school, I had some pretty good stats. I think in my senior year I hit over .600 with a lot of home runs."

Kittle may sound boastful when he talks about his ability, but, in fact, he is simply being honest. In high school, he hit 15 to 17 home runs a year—nearly one per game—and he would no more be falsely modest about his talent than he would exaggerate it.

For some reason, though, Kittle was not chosen by a big league team during the draft of amateur talent in June 1976, his senior year in high school. Partly because the interest in basketball is so strong in Indiana, baseball players are not scouted intensively there. Troxel says, "Really, the scouts had a bad book on him. They blew it."

But after graduating, Kittle went to an open tryout held by the Los Angeles Dodgers in nearby LaPorte, Indiana, and he apparently made quite an impression. "I showed 'em what I can do," he says. "I took a few swings and hit a bunch of balls over the fence. I played shortstop that day, caught, and played the outfield, all in the same game. They figured I was pretty versatile, and a couple of days later I signed a contract." It was July 5, 1976, and it looked like Ron Kittle finally had his ticket out of Gary.

It wasn't, unfortunately, quite so easy. By the time the Dodgers signed Kittle, they had filled the rosters of their teams in the lower minor leagues with players chosen in the draft. Kittle was told to wait until the next season to begin his professional career, so, for the time being, he took up construction work.

He worked alongside his father as an ironworker. "I was what they call a go-fer, a punk," he says. "You go around fetching up bolts, hooking up torches, gassing air bottles. Later I'd be working up on the beams, sometimes from four in the afternoon to six in the morning. The dirt would fly and my face would be black as graphite, but I made good money. If I weren't playing baseball, I'd still be doing that."

The following spring of 1977, Kittle made it to Dodgertown, the Dodgers' spring training complex in Vero Beach, Florida. "It was probably the most thrilling moment of my life," he says. "Practice was at nine o'clock each day, and I was probably at the door to the locker room at about six.

"I came in there in great shape and I did everything possible to make the team," he says. "I think I might have done everything a little bit too hard, you know, because it was the first time I'd experienced that caliber of baseball. I had a little bit of arm trouble in spring training, but that was just because I wasn't used to throwing every day. I was healthy until the season started."

Kittle was assigned to the Dodgers' Class A farm club in Clinton, Iowa, and some of the thrills turned into worries. "As soon as the season started—I guess it was about three or four days into the season—I began to have some severe headaches," he says. "It was a pain, but I figured a professional athlete has to go through aches and pains and play every day.

"Every time I went to the park, I was taking as many aspirin as I could to stop the pain. I had to play with it. I just wanted to play ball." The injury remained a mystery for most of the season. "I had it diagnosed by a couple of doctors and they just said it was a tension headache caused by tendinitis of the elbow. I took it for granted that it was, and I played hurt all season long."

Kittle played badly. He hit .189 with no home runs at Clinton, and spent two weeks on the disabled list before being demoted to the Dodgers' lowest-ranking farm club, the Lethbridge (Ont.) Dodgers of the Pioneer League. His stats improved slightly there, as he batted .250 with 7 home runs in 100 times at bat.

It was not a happy homecoming that fall in Gary, but Kittle felt a little better after he visited a couple of doctors. One of them, a neurologist, found after extensive testing that the young man had been playing with a couple of crushed vertebrae and pinched nerves in his neck.

Kittle still doesn't know how the injury occurred. "It was just a freak thing," he says. "They say it could happen anytime and anyplace." He was operated on that fall and spent the winter in a neck brace, resting and exercising a bit but doing nothing more strenuous than playing an occasional game of ping pong.

In the spring of 1978, Kittle returned to Dodgertown and was again assigned to Clinton. "I thought I was healthy, but I really didn't build my body up all that well," he says. He hit .143 and was released in early July.

Just two years after graduating from high school, Kittle was back home in Gary. "That's what was hard about it. I was eighteen years old, just starting out, and then I was out of baseball at twenty. It was pretty disappointing, but I couldn't give 100 percent. I knew it, and so did they."

While it was hard to go back home that summer, Kittle now thinks the injury and his subsequent release may have helped him in the long run—by calming him down a little and helping him to put baseball, and its place in his life, into perspective.

"You know, that accident might have happened for a reason," he says. "It made me realize that everything does not revolve around one thing—baseball. This is a glamour sport. It's a lot of fun. I wouldn't trade it for anything. But you've got your family and you've got different things in your life to do.

"My family stuck with me. I don't think they even cared that I hadn't made it. I think that was kind of nice." Still, he says, "I always had it in the back of my mind that I'd play again one day."

He went back to ironworking and joined a semipro baseball league on the southwest side of Chicago. He'd work eight or ten hours a day, and then play ball three night a week.

"I was doing a lot of heavy work in construction, building up my muscles, so I was in real good shape," he says. "I heard there were scouts who came out there off and on to see the ballplayers. I just said, heck, I'm going to go out there and show them what I've got."

He was spotted right away by a part-time scout who called in Billy Pierce, the former White Sox pitching great who now scouts for Chicago. Pierce checked Kittle out and arranged for him to come to Comiskey Park one night after work for a tryout. It was September 4, 1978, and the White Sox were home against Kansas City. The story of what happened during batting practice before the game that night has probably been embellished over time, but everyone agrees that Kittle was at his best when he was given a turn in the cage.

Here is his version: "They said, 'Okay, you hit.' So I'm in there, in the batting cage, and I hear in the background, 'Here's another guy wasting my time.' The first pitch they threw me, I completely missed. I heard somebody say, 'Just relax and hit the ball.'

"So I said to myself, heck, what do I have to lose? So I went up there and I just hit quite a few balls out of the ballyard and hit 'em hard, just about all over the place." One traveled at least 474 feet to clear the left field roof, and some observers say he hit seven of eleven balls out of the park. Whatever the real count, Bill Veeck, then the owner of the Sox, offered him a contract that night.

"I signed right away. I didn't even care what they were going to pay me. I was so glad to get back into baseball," Kittle recalls. "They gave me free tickets to stay and watch the ballgame, but I was so tired because I'd just put in an eight-hour day that I just went home and fell asleep."

The following spring, Kittle began his baseball career over again, this time at the training base of the White Sox in Sarasota, Florida. He was in better shape both physically and mentally than he had been two years earlier with the Dodgers.

"A lot of people don't get the first chance," he says. "I got two, and I wanted to take advantage of it." The White Sox, recognizing that his experience as a pro would put him ahead of other newly signed players, assigned Kittle to their Class AA team in Knoxville, Tennessee, of the Southern League, so his summer away from the game did not really slow his progress to the major leagues. But Kittle was still slow to develop as a player. Dividing his time between Knoxville and the Appleton (Wisc.) Foxes in the Class A Midwest League, he hit .267 with just 8 home runs and 38 runs batted in.

Perhaps more worrisome was the way he was moved from position to position by his managers. Kittle was used as a catcher, an outfielder, and frequently as a designated hitter.

The result was that he did not get enough work at any one spot to develop his fielding skills.

When the 1980 season began, Kittle returned to Appleton—back in the Midwest League where his career with the Dodgers had begun a full three years earlier. This time, though, he was ready to play. He hit over .300 with 12 homers and 56 RBIs in 61 games and was promoted, midway through the season, to the Glens Falls (N.Y.) White Sox of the Eastern League, where he continued to do well.

One day in late July, though, his season was ended by a new disabling injury. He dove for a baseball and tore the tendons in his thumb. "I had something going that year. I had 17 home runs so far," he says. "But, I thought, well, next year maybe I can get something going again if I play in a lot of games."

Through all the injuries and the setbacks, Kittle insists that he never became discouraged—especially the second time around. In comparison to his frustrations as a fledgling Dodger, he says, his troubles with the White Sox were minor and his spirits remained high. "It's just a lot of determination and a lot of heart. I just put a lot into it. I kept it in my heart that I want to be good," he says. "You've got to go out and give 100 percent, no matter what you do, whether it's this or drive a truck or play ping pong."

He never lost sight of his goal of reaching the big leagues. "You read in the box score and you see all these names up there, and somebody's got three or four hits or something like that, and you say, heck, one of these days I'm going to go up there and get three or four hits. You've got to keep that in your mind. Even if you strike out eight times in a row, you've got to go up there the ninth time and say, hey, I'm going to get a hit," he says.

Kittle's perseverance began to pay off in 1981. Back in Glens

Falls, his season began with a new problem—a bout with mononucleosis that forced him to miss twenty-one games in April and May. But he soon made up for the lost time. Kittle terrorized Eastern League pitchers that summer, clouting 40 home runs and knocking in 103 runs in 109 games. He batted .326, racked up a slugging percentage of .694, and after the season ended he was named the league's Most Valuable Player.

When the next spring came around, Kittle was invited to training camp with the big league club for the first time. He reported early to work on his fielding. The previous summer, he played just fifteen games in the outfield, spending the rest of the time as a designated hitter. His fielding had become the subject of as much talk as his awesome home runs. Teammates told of the time when Kittle ducked as a ball was flying toward his glove, giving the batter an inside the park home run. Another time he supposedly tripped over a bullpen pitching mound while chasing the ball, did a somersault, and barely recovered in time to hold the batter to a triple.

Kittle says the tales are exaggerated. But even though he hit .455 in training camp that spring with the White Sox, he was returned to the minors for one more year to improve his glove work. "Defense is not my strong point," Kittle said then. "I let my bat do the talking." He was assigned to the Edmonton Trappers of the Pacific Coast League, the Sox' top farm club, with instructions that he play in the outfield every day.

Kittle and Edmonton took to each other right away. He eyed the short left field porch in rickety Renfrew Park and began the season by slugging 11 home runs in his first 14 games. He hit two in one inning one night in late April, and smashed a couple of tape measure jobs that had coaches and writers shaking their heads in amazement. A columnist for the *Edmonton*

*Journal* was so impressed that he told his readers: "Get your butt down to our quaint little ballpark and glue it to a seat. . . . If you're even remotely a sports fan, you have to see Ronald Dale Kittle play baseball." The Trappers' president estimated that having Kittle on the team added $50,000 to the team's gate receipts over the season.

Few who came to watch Kittle were disappointed. Just seeing him swing the bat was impressive—his stroke smooth and powerful, his weight sliding easily from his back foot onto his front, and his wrist snapping right at the moment his bat makes contact with the ball—his form was so good. His numbers weren't bad either. Though he couldn't keep up the torrid pace at which he started the season, hitting 21 homers in his first 35 games, he was in the running for the league's triple crown all year. He also was rapidly approaching a magic mark—50 home runs—as the end of the season approached.

Number 50 came in the eighth inning of his last game as a Trapper, before an unusually big crowd of 4,234. "As soon as the ball left the bat, I was ecstatic," he said then. "I don't usually get too excited about a home run."* He tossed his helmet high in the air as he crossed home plate and was mobbed by his teammates.

To go along with the 50 homers and 144 RBIs, Kittle had scored 121 runs and amassed 355 total bases—all league-leading totals. He had a slugging percentage of .729 and a batting average of .345. He was named the league's MVP and the minor league player of the year by Topp's Chewing Gum and the *Sporting News*.

"I had kind of the season I expected," he said at the time.

---

* *Edmonton Journal,* September 2, 1982.

"I'll be honest. I was going for the big numbers all season." Looking ahead, he said, "I don't think anything is going to stop me now."

He arrived in Chicago for the last month of the 1982 season, appeared in a few games as a pinch hitter, and hit .247 with 7 RBIs. "I got a little taste of it, but I didn't do as well as I wanted to," he says. "It did me good just to get used to the atmosphere up here, to accept the role of a major leaguer, to know what the job is."

On the second-to-last day of the season, Kittle hit his first big league home run. It came off pitcher Frank Viola of the Minnesota Twins at the Metrodome in Minneapolis. "I wanted that first one just to get a little pressure off me," he says. "Because if you come up with some credentials from the minor leagues, you're going to be playing with a lot of pressure. The media coverage is going to be a lot stronger, and if a guy's not able to accept it, that's going to hurt him in the long run."

If Kittle thought there was a lot of media coverage that September, he must have been surprised in the following spring. During training camp and the first weeks of the season, he is the subject of countless newspaper stories and extensive television coverage as well as a profile in *Sports Illustrated.* Kittle has no trouble handling the attention. He is willing to answer question after question with a smile and charms reporters with stories about his rise to the top, his roots in the steel mills, and his mom's German chocolate cake.

The more difficult tests for Kittle come on the field. The White Sox have lost slugging left fielder Steve Kemp to the New York Yankees, leaving Kittle, fellow rookie Greg Walker, and veteran Tom Paciorek to fight over jobs at first base and in left field.

On Opening Day in Texas, Walker plays first, Paciorek plays left, and Kittle sits on the bench. But Kittle is unperturbed, saying, "It doesn't bother me. I'll get my playing time." The next day, he takes over left field and goes 0 for 3. When he picks up a single and a double in the final game of the series, there is nothing to celebrate. The Sox have dropped three in a row to the Rangers.

The next stop is Detroit, and Kittle strikes out three times in the first game there. But he rebounds impressively two days later to collect his first home run of 1983. It comes on Sunday, April 10, against Jack Morris of the Tigers with two men on in the first inning, and the ball is hit so far and so hard that it careens around an entrance ramp in the upper deck a half-dozen times before rolling to a stop. It is pure Kittle.

Four innings later, Kittle comes up again with runners at the corners. Morris—a respected right-hander who is rough on right-handed hitters like Kittle—goes ahead in the count, 0–2, but the young rookie stands his ground. He takes a fastball and then a curve, both inside for balls, to even the count at 2–2, and fouls off another fastball. Then comes the kind of delivery that has fooled many a slugger—a curveball, dipping down and away out of the strike zone. It is the turning point of the confrontation, and Kittle takes the pitch for ball three.

"The key is," LaRussa says later, "if you can get him to swing at a bad pitch, you're going to get him out just like you're going to get every hitter out. But if he makes them throw the ball over the plate, then he's got a chance to hit it hard."

Kittle gets his chance on the payoff pitch from Morris, and hits it just hard enough to drop into short left field for a single that drives in his fourth run of the afternoon and sends the pitcher to the showers. So long, Jack Morris. Hello, Ron Kittle.

It is the start of a memorable week for the rookie. In

Chicago's home opener against Baltimore on Tuesday, Kittle homers again and drives in two runs in a losing effort. Two days later, he proves that performance was no fluke by driving in six runs with a 410-foot three-run homer, a two-run single, and a sacrifice fly as the White Sox win a 12–11 slugfest in freezing temperatures.

Kittle jokes afterward that he had an advantage over the other players on the field. "I played in this kind of weather in Edmonton all last season. I was just trying to chip the frost off my toes," he says.*

He caps his week on Sunday against the Tigers by slamming a two-run homer in the first inning off Jerry Ujdur to spark the Sox to a 6–1 win. The blast gives him 4 homers and 14 RBIs, tops in the American League. He is really rolling.

The following week is memorable, but for an entirely different reason—Kittle is terrible, plunging into his first slump of the season. His big swing all of a sudden seems too big, too hard, as he swings through fastballs and over dipping curves. Perhaps because his string of home runs has made him overconfident, Kittle seems to be going for the fences.

He goes 0 for 15, and it isn't because he is hitting balls hard that are caught. He strikes out seven times before finally ending the streak with an infield single one afternoon. The Sox, meanwhile, drop three games in a row.

The slump is no surprise, given the tendency of most free-swinging sluggers to combine their awesome home run power with a frightful number of strikeouts. The all-time major league strikeout leader is Reggie Jackson, who took the title away from Mickey Mantle. Both were home run and strikeout kings.

---

* *Chicago Tribune,* April 15, 1983.

Frank Howard, a formidable slugger who later managed the New York Mets, has watched many young power hitters come and go. Howard follows Kittle's progress during 1983 as he tutors Met rookie Darryl Strawberry, a promising young power hitter and the closest thing to Kittle in the National League.

"We all have peaks and valleys in this game, but usually with the big strong guys their peaks and their valleys are more severe," Howard says. "Slumps aren't going to be as deep or as prolonged with an average hitter as they are with the guys who do a little business with those cheap seats." Howard says slumping power hitters "drive a lot of coaches and managers up the wall because you have to suffer with them a lot of times. The [Rocky] Colavitos, the Gorman Thomases, the [Harmon] Killebrews, they may go two or three weeks when they don't hit a home run. You have to be a little more patient with them."

When the slumping power hitter is a rookie, the biggest danger can be self-doubt. Kittle's hitless week or Strawberry's painfully slow start naturally invite comparisons with such sluggers as Steve Bilko or Joe Hauser—the guys who could hit 50 or 60 homers in the minors but not in the big time. But young players cannot afford to question their ability.

"I'd strike out three times and hit into a double play, and I think you just have to say, 'I'm going to leave it here behind me,' " Howard says. "But when you're young, you'll carry that into the next night's game, and the next thing you know, instead of punching out three times and hitting a double play ball, you're punching out four times. If you're down on yourself, you're just going to sink deeper and deeper into that little valley you're in."

So Kittle's prolonged slump in April provides the first test this season of both the patience of his manager and coaches and the strength of his own self-confidence. When Rick Sutcliffe, a tough right-handed pitcher for the Cleveland Indians, takes the mound against Chicago on Sunday, April 24, Kittle is not in the lineup for the first time since Opening Day. LaRussa is careful to say that Kittle is just being rested and will return to the lineup soon: "He's not benched. He's just been struggling and I wanted to experiment with the lineup a little bit."

LaRussa says that handling a slumping player is one of the thorniest problems a manager faces. "Sometimes you rest them, sometimes you give them extra work, sometimes you stay with them. It depends.

"If he needs your confidence by keeping him in the lineup, you do that. If he needs to rest because he's really struggling and going backwards, then you rest him. Everybody struggles through the years, no matter how good a hitter you are. So you just kind of watch for it, get a feel for it, and when the time comes, you use one of the remedies that are available."

Charlie Lau, the Sox batting coach, also resists the temptation to tinker with Kittle. During Kittle's slump, Lau gives the rookie a few tips to help prepare himself at the plate but decides that the mechanics of his swing are sound. "When most good hitters go to home plate, people don't realize it but they have little habits that they go through that assure balance and assure proper alignment," Lau says. "His swing is a good swing. You don't mess around with a good swing."

While Lau helps Kittle with his physical approach to the plate, the veteran batting coach can do nothing but marvel at the rookie's mental approach—especially coming off a bad day or a slump. Kittle, he says, seems to have the confidence and security that a good power hitter needs. "They've got to be able to handle, when they don't hit a home run, people screaming at them and writers saying what in the hell happened." He says of Kittle, "I think he can strike out five times and still have a secure feeling that he's going to pop the next one."

For many ballplayers, finding that kind of inner strength is especially difficult because their defeats—unlike the failures of people in most occupations—are so public. "You can't hide 'em. You read about them the next day. The public sees them on TV. They see it as fans in the ballpark," Lau says.

Kittle isn't quite so philosophical. He says the first slump didn't bother him because he understood what caused it, and he was sure it would be just a matter of time before he could correct it. "I knew what I was doing wrong at the plate," he says. "I was overswinging. It was just a little adjustment right there. When you overswing, your head goes up and you pull out and you don't see the ball well. It's just a bad habit."

But what Kittle could breezily dismiss as "just a bad habit" might have grown into a much more worrisome problem for a less secure player. Especially when things are going bad, some players make too many adjustments. Often a hitter will press too hard at just the time when he ought to be relaxing more. Kittle seems to understand this. "That's the secret of this game. . . . You want to do everything hard, but to do it right you have to be relaxed and well-balanced."

Staying relaxed is difficult, though, given the pressure to win in the big leagues. Kittle calls that the biggest difference between playing in Edmonton and playing in Chicago. "Up here, you want to win every day, day in and day out. The minor leagues are just training for the major league level. There's more stress up here on winning all the time."

But Kittle says he puts all that out of his mind as he approaches the plate. "I don't worry," he says. "If the guy's throwing 500 miles an hour or 100 miles an hour, I just try to go up there and look at the situation and see what I have to do."

It is one of the paradoxes of baseball that a player must be intensely determined to succeed, but at the same time must be relaxed and unafraid of failure. Kittle says the pressure to succeed does not affect him, even during the bad times. "If I went up there and I struck out fifty times in a row, I'd probably throw something around the locker room," he says with a laugh. "But if I did that bad, I probably wouldn't be playing."

After he is rested for a couple of days and his first slump ends, Kittle returns to the lineup and shows no sign of lost confidence. On his first day back, he collects two hits against Milwaukee, and soon the home runs begin to fly again. Pitchers try different things against him but none seem to work consistently. In one game in Chicago, Kittle is fooled by an off-speed pitch from Frank Tanana of the Texas Rangers and swings with one hand. The result: home run. In Boston's Fenway Park, Kittle sends a fastball over the plate from Bruce Hurst onto the screen in left and then does the same with a high changeup from John Tudor. In New York, Kittle clouts a tremendous home run off Dave Righetti and then hits a Goose Gossage fastball so hard that it nearly knocks over third baseman Graig Nettles.

"I don't think there's going to be a book on him," LaRussa predicts. "He has hit fastballs out of the park. He has hit breaking balls out of the park. He has hit a changeup against the wall. He's capable of handling all pitches. It's just a question of seeing the ball and having a certain amount of discipline."

By mid-June, Kittle's 15 home runs and 45 RBIs are good enough to be leading the league. The following month, Kittle is the only rookie to be chosen to the American League team for the All-Star game in Comiskey Park. During the second half of the season, his run production slows down and his batting average dips. By then, though, some of his teammates who had slumped during the spring are getting hot, and the team is riding atop the standings in the league's Western Division.

Perhaps the most pleasant surprise for the Sox as the season progresses is Kittle's play in the outfield. While he will never win a Gold Glove award for his defense, there are no more jokes about how he is feared by every pitcher in the league—by the opposing pitchers when he hits and by his own team's pitchers when he fields.

"If there's been one real good plus for us, it's the fact that he's played left field above average so far this season," says LaRussa. "That shows me he's a good athlete."

"Everyone needs to work at a position until he masters it. I'm starting to feel comfortable in the outfield," Kittle says.

In fact, Kittle is feeling very comfortable with every aspect of big league life. He has friends on the team and enjoys the travel, and he basks in the attention that he gets whenever the White Sox arrive in a new city. He buys new clothes, moves out of his parents' house, and finds an apartment of his own in northwest Indiana.

Kittle is finally where he wants to be—in the lineup every day for his home town team as they fight for the pennant. The crowds flock to Comiskey Park, and not a few of them gather in the left field stands to cheer Kittle. Their cheering unnerved him at first. "When I first came up here, I think I heard every word everybody said in the stands. I wasn't used to having people behind me, because in the minor leagues there were no outfield stands. It was just a different atmosphere," he recalls. Now Kittle is used to it. "I can hardly hear it anymore," he says.

Kittle has silenced other voices, too: the voices of critics who said he could never play the outfield, the voices of skeptics who scoffed at his minor league achievements, the voices of those who said he struck out too often. Most important of all, in his struggle to find the right stance—both physical and mental—Ron Kittle has quieted the voices of self-doubt that proved to be the undoing of so many rookies. He has waited too long for this season to waste his chance now.

# 5 On the Fringe: *Bill Almon of the Oakland A's*

The 1983 baseball season is not yet two months old, and it is already shaping up as another strange year for Bill Almon. He gets up each morning and goes to the ballpark without knowing what role he will be called on to play—or even whether he will play at all.

This Sunday, May 29, is typical. Almon and the rest of the A's are in New York to wrap up a three-game series against the New York Yankees. The first two games of the series have been productive for Almon. Because New York used left-handed pitchers, Almon, who bats right-handed, was pleased to find himself in the starting lineup for both games. He played third base and shortstop on Friday and right field on Saturday, collecting a single, a double, and a run batted in in the two games. His batting average—a solid .282—is among the best on the A's.

On Sunday morning, Almon is sitting in a corner of the visitors clubhouse at Yankee Stadium and putting on his green and gold uniform when he spots Jackie Moore, the first base coach for the A's, taping the lineup card to the wall. He yells across the clubhouse: "Jackie, am I playing?" The answer is not the one he wants to hear. Moore says he is listed first in the

A's
OAKLAND

category of "Extra Men," and Almon shakes his head. "Figures," he says. "Right-handed pitcher."

The Yankees start right-hander Jay Howell that afternoon, and, as it turns out, Almon is the first man off the Oakland bench when Howell is relieved by lefty Rudy May. He is asked to pinch hit in the fifth inning with runners at second and third and two out. May strikes him out.

It has been that kind of a season for Bill Almon—a season of uncertainty as he has been moved in and out of the lineup and shifted from position to position, depending on who else is available, who is pitching for the opposition, and—a sometimes worrisome factor—how he has been playing lately. This is nothing new to Almon, who at thirty has spent seven curious seasons in the major leagues. He has played for five teams: the San Diego Padres, Montreal Expos, New York Mets, Chicago White Sox, and now the A's.

A high school and college sensation, Almon was touted as a can't-miss star at shortstop when he signed with the San Diego Padres in 1974. But instead of pursuing stardom, he has had to struggle throughout his career to prove that he belongs in the big leagues.

Some baseball people classify Almon as a utility player—a man available to fill in at a variety of positions, usually when one of the regulars in the starting lineup is hurt or needs a rest. The classic utility man is an adequate fielder, a poor hitter, and a cheerful fellow who adapts to his role, which, while not glamorous, is important to the team. He is the guy who arrives for spring training with a catcher's mitt under his arm, hoping that the ability to play yet another position will prolong his career.

Almon is not really that type. He wants very badly to play

every day, and, in fact, he appears in too many games to be playing the classic utility role. Nor does he fit the good-field, no-hit stereotype of the benchwarmer. Almon, in fact, is a good hitter. When he does play, he sometimes bats third in the line-up, a spot reserved for a strong offensive man. And unlike the classic utility man, his fielding is suspect. Probably the biggest problem of his career has been his reputation as an inconsistent defensive player.

But Almon, for all his hitting ability, cannot break into Oakland's everyday starting lineup. He didn't play at all, for example, on Opening Day and only appeared in his first game a couple of days later as a pinch hitter. He didn't get his first start—or his first base hit—until Oakland had played six games and the season was more than a week old. His first chance to play every day came in May, when the A's regular third base-man, Carney Lansford, sprained his wrist.

What is surprising about all this is that neither Almon, an intelligent and well-spoken man with a pleasant personality, nor A's manager Steve Boros, who is just as smart and articulate and affable, are able to shed much light on what is happening to Almon. His role simply isn't easy to define.

In several conversations during the summer, Almon never seems angry or upset about the way he is moved in and out of the lineup in various positions. He admits, however, that he is surprised by the way things are going for him this season.

"This year's been more unusual than ever," he says. "I've played more positions than I ever have, and I've actually played a lot of games." By the time of the weekend series in Yankee Stadium, Almon has batted 108 times and appeared in all but eight of Oakland's forty-five games. For that, he is grateful.

"When they told me at the end of spring training that I

wasn't going to be the starting shortstop, if you told me that I'd have more than 100 at bats at this point in the season, I'd have told you that you were crazy," he says. "So I'm really pleased just to be playing as much as I am."

Still, Almon believes that he would be a better player if he had the chance to play the same position, day in and day out, as a member of the starting lineup. His career history seems to bear him out. Entering the 1983 season, Almon's lifetime batting average, even taking into account the times when he was a part-time player, was .258—not bad for a middle infielder. He hit .301 as the regular shortstop for the Chicago White Sox in 1981, and he hit close to .300 during several other periods when he was given a starting role. He hasn't, however, been nearly as effective as a part-timer.

"Whenever I have played on an everyday basis, I have shown that I could produce and play," he says. "That's one thing I kept preaching to clubs. When you take all my numbers together, they're average. But when I play every day, here are my numbers and they're good major league stats."

Steve Boros, Oakland's forty-six-year-old rookie manager, can sympathize with Almon. Boros played seven seasons in the majors with Detroit, Cincinnati, and the Chicago Cubs, sometimes bouncing back and forth between the majors and the minor leagues. "I was never really at a point where my career was a good enough career where I knew that they would just give me the job and I didn't have to worry about whether I got off to a bad start or not," Boros says.

Boros is pleased with the way Almon has adjusted to his many roles this season. He is used to relieve one rookie in right field and another at shortstop, to play first base and right field against some left-handed pitchers, and occasionally to serve as the designated hitter. Lansford's injury gives him playing time at third, too.

"That's the thing that's remarkable," Boros says. "He's adapted to all the positions we've put him in, and so far we've used him at five—left field, right field, shortstop, third base, and first base. He's got quite a few at-bats. I work at trying to find ways to get him into the lineup."

Boros is also glad that Almon, unlike some players, can sit on the bench without making trouble. "When he's not playing, he's right there cheerleading and encouraging the other players. So he's really been an asset to our ballclub on and off the field."

Boros realizes, though, that shuffling a player like Almon in and out of the lineup, while perhaps helpful to the team, is probably not the best thing for the player himself. "It can't be a good situation for him mentally," Boros admits. "I know because, in my career, I was mainly an extra man and I had to do the same sort of thing. It's got to be distracting, not knowing what position you're going to play when you come to the ballpark—if you're going to play at all."

While Almon seems sure that he has the talent to succeed in the major leagues, the confusion about his role cannot help but affect his play. It must also plant doubts in his mind about his ability and his future in the big leagues. Many professional baseball players are plagued by such doubts, and, for some, insecurity about their future becomes a fact of life. While fans, naturally, read and hear more about baseball's top stars and most successful players, big league clubhouses are filled with players who wonder whether this season will be their last. The Pete Roses and Reggie Jacksons are far outnumbered in the world of baseball by the Bill Almons and the Bob Bailors and the Kurt Bevacquas—part-timers or utility men who must earn their jobs each year.

In the minor leagues, of course, insecurity is a way of life; success at one level is no guarantee of anything, and making the big leagues seems to require just the right mix of ability and luck. For some players, though, hanging on in the majors is as tough as getting there. The average player spends five years in the big leagues—barely enough to qualify for a pension. Ex–big leaguers who need a few more months to qualify pack the rosters of top minor league teams.

Almon has already qualified for a pension, and his goal is not just to hang on in the majors but to find a secure starting role somewhere. That goal, however, is becoming more difficult to reach with each passing season.

As a shortstop, Almon's chances of winning a starting berth seem slim. No matter what the statistics show, big league teams in need of a new starting shortstop rarely turn to an older player who has been rejected elsewhere. While some teams have considered using Almon as an outfielder or third baseman, it is difficult for even an established player to win a starting role at a new position in mid-career.

It seems more likely that Almon may soon have to put aside the question of whether he can win a starting job and replace it with a more troubling one—the question of how many more years he will be able to remain in the big leagues.

Such worries were far from Bill Almon's mind on the afternoon of June 5, 1974—a day when he could claim, with considerable justification, that he was the best high school or college baseball player in America. The San Diego Padres, by compiling the worst record in baseball the previous season, had "won" the right to select the first player in the annual draft of amateur baseball players. They chose Almon, a high school and college superstar who was then a twenty-one-year-old junior at Brown University. No one could remember a time when a kid from the East—from the Ivy League, no less—had been the first pick in the draft, an honor that usually goes to a player from a top baseball school in the sunbelt.

The Padres, though, wanted the lean 6 feet 3 inch, 180 pound shortstop who the scouts said could do it all. Almon could hit, run, field, and throw. One scout said he could range deep into the hole to his right, set himself, and fire the ball to first as well as any big league shortstop.

It was a happy day for the Almon clan—parents Ted and Gloria, sons Ted, Bob, John, and Bill, and daughters Mary and Anne-Marie. The family was big enough, and athletic enough, to form sides for a pickup game of nearly any sport, and the kids grew up playing sports, sports, and more sports. "I started playing baseball when I was about five years old with my brothers and sisters and other kids in the neighborhood," Bill says. "We played in our back yard, and we just about played constantly."

Like many major leaguers, Bill had a sports-minded father who encouraged and guided him. Ted Almon played baseball as a young man and then played in the army during World War II with several big leaguers, including Alvin Dark and Ted Williams. But he was too old when the war ended to pursue a baseball career. "I don't think it's anything he regrets," Bill says, "but he's awfully proud of me because he can sort of live it through me. He really loves the game." When Bill and younger brother John, who later spent three years in the minor leagues, played in Little League and Babe Ruth League, Ted Almon coached their teams.

"Probably the most important thing he taught us was attitude," Bill says. He still remembers what his dad always told him. "You're going to give it your best effort. You're going to go out every day and try hard."

Bill was a natural athlete to whom all sports came easily. He was also a fine student, graduating near the top of his class at Warwick High School in Rhode Island. For a while, it looked like basketball might be his sport. He was the top scorer in Rhode Island in his senior year, and several colleges offered him basketball scholarships. But Almon was even better at baseball. After he batted over .400, pitched brilliantly, and made the all-state team for three consecutive years, every major league team scouted him, and some clubs wanted to make him an early round draft choice.

He elected instead to attend Brown, a fine university in Providence, close to home. "I needed a little more maturity, and the college education was important," he says. He studied hard, cramming three and a half years of work into three years.

By the time his junior year ended in 1974, Almon had captured fifteen offensive records at the school, batted .357, and been named an All-American. After the *Sporting News* chose him as the college baseball player of the year, no one was surprised when he became the number one choice.

He and his father decided not to use an agent to handle his first contract, and it turned out they didn't need one. San Diego offered a bonus of close to $100,000, and the Almons took it. They also negotiated an unusual clause—one that looked good at the time but, in retrospect, may have been a mistake. Almon got the Padres to agree to bring him up to the big leagues for a trial the following September, only four months after he left school.

"I figured I was twenty-one and definitely old enough to try it, so let's get a taste of it right away," he recalls. "It was just a chance to get there, meet the guys, travel a little bit, and see what the life was like."

He began his pro career with the Hawaiian Islanders, San Diego's top farm club in the Class AAA Pacific Coast League. Few players are introduced to pro ball at such a high level, and Almon's first manager at Hawaii, Roy Hartsfield, decided the youngster wasn't ready. So, for a couple of months, Almon rode the bench—a strange introduction to the game for such a touted prospect.

Part of the problem was that the Padres had a loose arrangement with the Hawaii team, and Hartsfield was under pressure from the local owners to win. "He wasn't inclined to play a youngster out of college," Almon says. "He didn't have any confidence in me. When you think about it, you can't blame the guy."

With just 36 at-bats as the season passed its halfway mark, Almon was getting restless. He asked the Padres to send him down one level, to their Class AA team in Alexandria, Texas, so he could get some playing time. He got the time but not the results he wanted.

"I didn't do very well, mainly because I hadn't played in a long time and because I put a little pressure on myself being a number one pick and wanting to do extra well," he says. "It was a whole new life and everything was coming together at the same time."

Nevertheless, because of the contract, Almon and his .186 batting average arrived in San Diego in September. Remarkably, he performed well, hitting .316 in 16 games. He also fell in love with life in the big leagues. "It was everything I expected and more," he says. "You travel first class everywhere—going from town to town, a couple of days here, a couple of days there. At the time, I was single and that's what I was up for. It was very exciting."

His strange first year as a pro had ended on an upbeat note, but his few weeks in the big leagues may have raised his expectations a little too high. He played well in an instructional league over the winter and arrived at the Yuma, Arizona, spring training base of the Padres in February 1975, fully expecting to make the team. The Padres' shortstop at the time was a journeyman named Enzo Hernandez.

When Almon had a good spring, he felt even better about his chances. Then came a shocker. "It was the last day of spring training," he says. "The manager, John McNamara, called me into his office and said I had a good spring and everything, but they just felt I needed some time to play every day in the minor leagues. They said it would be best for me. I objected and I asked for some reasons. They just felt they could make do with what they had."

The Padres' decision made perfect sense, given Almon's inexperience. But he had trouble accepting it. "Basically, that was the first time I had ever faced defeat in baseball—meaning being cut from a club or anything. This was the first setback, and I couldn't really understand why they wanted to hold me back," he says.

He returned to Hawaii, but not in the right state of mind to play good baseball. "What I did was, mentally, I let that affect me. I was devastated and I didn't recover from it. It just ate away at me. I couldn't believe it. I couldn't handle it. I went out there every day and outwardly I was the same person, but inwardly it was just something that was eating away at me."

His performance suffered. He hit just .228 and led all shortstops in the league in errors with 48. Returning to spring training the next year with a more realistic attitude, Almon was able to accept it when the Padres asked him to return to Hawaii for his third season in a row.

"I was more mature and I understood the situation, and I just said: I'm going to go out and play and do a good job; I've got to play here in Hawaii, this is where I am, and so I might as well do well," he remembers. His batting average climbed to .291, he cut down on his errors, and the team won the championship for the second straight year. "I finally hit my stride," he says.

In the spring of 1977, the Padres decided that Almon was finally ready for the majors, and they made him their starting shortstop. He got off to a slow start, feeling uncertain at bat and in the field, but soon he began to relax and his play improved.

"From Memorial Day on, the season just built. Everything—all my stats—just had an upward flow. It was very satisfying. I became very comfortable in my job, and I felt I'd made a good stride in establishing myself in baseball," he says.

Almon finished the season with a .261 batting average, and he led the league in sacrifice bunts with 20. His fielding was still thought by some to be a problem—while his range was excellent, he led league shortstops in errors with 41. But it had been a satisfying year, and Almon and his wife Kathy—his high school girlfriend whom he had married two years earlier—settled into a house and made some good friends in San Diego.

The following spring training, though, brought a new and unexpected problem for Almon—a brilliant young shortstop named Osborne Earl Smith. Ozzie Smith, then twenty-three, had played just one year in the minor leagues, but he was a spectacular fielder with all the poise and self-confidence of a veteran. He dazzled the Padres' managers and coaches during the spring and won the shortstop's job.

Almon was left without a position. First, manager Alvin Dark spent the spring trying him at second base. When Dark was fired before the season began, new skipper Roger Craig installed him at third. The change raised two immediate questions: could he field the new position, and could he hit well enough to play third?

"I really had never played there, and I didn't really get much instruction on how to play there," Almon says. "I was thrown in, and it was baptism by fire. . . . It was quite difficult." Almon didn't embarrass himself, but, even today, he is not comfortable at third.

His hitting posed a different kind of problem. The Padres had worked extensively with Almon to make him a slap hitter who bats out of a crouch and sprays the ball to all fields—the type of hitter you often find at short. But the third base position, which demands less speed and agility and defensive talent than shortstop, tends to be reserved for stronger and more powerful hitters. (The reason, essentially, is that the pool of players who have the defensive talent to play third is bigger, allowing teams to demand more offense from the third baseman.)

This worried Almon. He recalls telling the Padres: "Look, offensively I'm not a home run hitter. You want a third baseman, but I hope you don't expect me to be a home run hitter. You've all along in the minors taught me just the opposite." They replied: "No, no, no, we don't expect that."

For a couple of months, things worked out. His fielding was erratic but his bat was hot, and two months into the season he had played all 50 games and led the team in batting average (.291), hits (54), and doubles (12). He was happy, and San Diegans were taking a liking to him. He did a few TV ads for local stores and was working on an endorsement deal with a chain of pizza parlors.

Craig, though, wasn't impressed. "They came to me about that time," Almon recalls, "and they said they wanted to start platooning me because I wasn't producing enough runs offensively. From that point on, I was platooned at third base, which was not what I wanted to do.

"All my stats started to slip slowly because I wasn't getting up half as much as I was before, and it was hard to stay sharp," he says. Almon collected fewer hits in the last four months of the season than he had in the first two, and his average slid to .252 by the season's end.

Almon had enjoyed baseball immensely during his rookie year, but several years would pass before he would enjoy it again. He was too young to be a part-time player, he felt, and definitely capable of playing every day in the big leagues. However, he had been given the label of utility man during his second season in San Diego, and it stuck.

At the time, the Padres praised Almon for being flexible when they used him at various positions. But he came to feel that his versatility had backfired. "It starts out as a blessing, but then it can be a hindrance," he says. "I played at lot of positions, but I really didn't get that many opportunities to play. I was mopping up at the end of games." Often Almon was the last extra man to get into a game because the manager had saved him, knowing he could go in whether the opening was at second, short, or third. It was a role he found hard to accept.

"There are a very few people in this game who are designed

to play just once in a while. They perform great for a short period of time and if they keep playing they don't do well. But if you rest them, then they come back in and they play great," Almon says.

"I'm just the opposite," he observes. "I have to play every day or close to every day to be productive. I'm the first one to admit it."

Forced to adjust to a part-time role, he developed little techniques to keep himself busy on the bench and be prepared for the now-and-then opportunities that came up. "I showed up at the ballpark with the attitude that I was going to be in the lineup. Most of the time I wasn't, but I tried to go through my workout and everything as if I was going to be playing. I'd try to keep as sharp as possible.

"The hardest thing I found was sitting down on the bench for five, six, seven innings, and then having to go into a ballgame. It's hard to get yourself not so much mentally prepared but to get going again physically. You've sat down for an hour and a half or even two hours. It's a cold start.

"Between innings, I used to try to run up the runways and do as much stretching as I could. Then, when I went into a game, I tried to put the situation in my mind that the game was just starting and this was the first inning. I almost tried to trick myself."

The best statistical measure of his growing frustration was his number of at-bats. Almon had 613 at-bats in his rookie year, 405 in his sophomore season, and 198 in 1979. He found himself caught in a cycle that was extremely difficult to break: the fewer games he played, the more his performance suffered, and the fewer chances he had to play.

It became almost impossible for him to maintain the relaxed

and confident attitude that is essential to success in baseball. "I put a little pressure on myself when I did get my starts because I felt it was an opportunity to show them that I could play," Almon says. "I wanted to take advantage of all the opportunities I got because they were few and far between."

The pressure he placed on himself, however, produced just the opposite effect. "You just sit there and then, when you do get the chance, you haven't played enough and you don't feel quite as confident in yourself as you should," he said. "Probably if you just relaxed and went out there you'd be close to as good as you could be, but, you know, there's always that thing in the back of your mind, have I been doing enough extra work? Or, I haven't been playing, so maybe I'm not as sharp as I could be.

"There's always that little itty bit of a doubt that hopefully you can dispel, but a lot of times it's there and it does affect you."

Disgruntled, Almon did not get along with Craig, his manager. Almon had asked to be traded in 1978, his first season as a part-timer, but he didn't get his wish until after another disappointing season in 1979. That fall, Almon and first baseman–outfielder Dan Briggs were dealt to the Expos for second baseman Dave Cash.

Kathy Almon gave birth to their first child, a boy, a few weeks later, and the new baby and the trade together made the winter a happy one. Dick Williams, the skipper of the Expos, was encouraging when he called to welcome Almon to Montreal, and Almon figured that the team would not have traded for him unless they wanted to use him. Plus, Montreal was a young team and a contender, not a second-division expansion club like the Padres. The trade, it seemed, would present Almon with just what he needed—a chance to make a fresh start.

Almon had a great spring, hitting over .300. But the Expos decided to stick with their shortstop–second base combination of Chris Speier and Rodney Scott, and as the season began Almon was again relegated to the role of extra man. Then, on the eve of the All-Star Game, Montreal needed to find a place on its twenty-five-man roster for third baseman Larry Parrish, who had recovered from an injury. They asked Almon to report to their Triple A farm team in Denver. He refused. As a player with three years of experience in the major leagues, Almon exercised his option not to report and instead became a free agent. He returned to his home in East Greenwich, Rhode Island, and called every team in the big leagues. It was touchy for a day or two—the big league executives were busy at meetings during the All-Star break—but soon his phone started to ring and three or four teams made offers.

He joined the New York Mets, a team with even fewer good players than San Diego but one where he felt he would have a chance to play. But his bad fortune continued when he sprained his back and injured some tendons in his throwing hand. He got some playing time—Doug Flynn, the Mets' regular second baseman, had a broken wrist and couldn't play at all—but his performance continued to slide. He batted .170 in 48 games with the Mets and ended the season with an anemic .193 average—by far his worst as a big leaguer.

The following December, Mets General Manager Frank Cashen called with more bad news—Almon was being released from his contract. Some six and a half years after being the first pick in the draft, his career seemed near its end. Bill Almon had been told by three teams that they didn't want him any more.

It was time for a family meeting. Leaving baseball was

seriously considered; Almon had just finished work on his degree at Brown by taking courses in the off-season, and there was a job waiting for him in the family's medical supply business. But he decided, with the support of the family, to give it one more try, and he began by calling Haywood Sullivan, general manager of the Boston Red Sox. Like most Rhode Islanders, the Almons were Red Sox fans, and Boston had just traded its shortstop, Rick Burleson.

Sullivan said no thanks, but another local connection came through. Roland Hemond, the general manager of the Chicago White Sox, is from Central Falls, Rhode Island, and a local White Sox scout urged him to consider Almon. Hemond began getting calls from other friends back home who had followed Almon's career, and the Chicago general manager decided to invite him to spring training.

When Almon arrived in Sarasota, Florida, with a minor league contract and a chance to try out for the White Sox, he was well-prepared. He had spent the winter "un-learning" the batting style and stance that he had been taught by the Padres, and returning to the more upright stance he had used in college. He figured that he was about to get his last shot in the majors and decided to do things his own way. The Padres had taught Almon to be a slap hitter—to look for gaps in the defense and then try to direct the ball through them. They also had him hit out of a crouch, like most infielders do. But, Almon says now, "I can't hit that way.

"So what I did was scrap everything I knew and had been taught professionally and just reverted back to my college batting stance. I worked all that winter at getting back into that style and perfecting it again.

"My theory then and now is just hit the ball as hard as I can, no matter where it goes. I just want to drive it someplace. It'll find its own holes and make its own hits."

Armed with his old stance and blessed with some good luck, Almon made the White Sox. While he had performed well during the spring, he seemed a likely candidate for assignment to the minors until, in the final days of training camp, the White Sox' top two shortstops, Todd Cruz and Greg Pryor, were injured. The job went to Almon because there was no one else to take it. But Manager Tony LaRussa assured Cruz that, once he was ready to play, the starting job would be his again.

Two months later, LaRussa had to eat his words. Almon was off to his best start ever and it was Cruz, not the newcomer, who was headed for the minors. Somehow Almon had found his confidence again—and with it his .300 average and fielding skills.

"I was relaxed the whole time," Almon says. "I had some days when I didn't get any hits and it never bothered me. I had gone out, and I had done my best, and it was all I could do."

His happiest summer had many good moments, starting with a two-run single against the Red Sox—the team that didn't want him—on the first weekend of the season. He was leading the league in hitting at one point with a gaudy .338 average. He was stealing bases and fielding his position smoothly.

An odd moment came on Friday night, May 8, when Almon muffed a routine ground ball that was hit right at him. The scoreboard flashed "E" for error—and the crowd of 42,000 at Comiskey Park burst into applause. The reason? Almon had handled his first 114 fielding chances flawlessly, which had been noted by the newspapers since his defensive ability had so often been questioned. The fans were saying thanks for doing so well for so long. "That was really a surprise," he said then.

The only disappointment for Almon was that his best major league season was interrupted by the sixty-day baseball strike. Still, he ended the year with a fine .301 batting average, tops among American League shortstops, and the Chicago baseball writers voted him the team's most valuable player.

For the first time in years, Almon felt like a big leaguer again. "I not only proved it to myself, but I proved to a lot of people that I deserved to still be playing and I had the ability to help a team on an everyday basis," he says.

That fall, figuring that his value to the team had grown substantially, Almon did the natural thing—he asked for a big raise. The White Sox offered a raise, but a smaller one. Trouble soon followed.

Baseball teams and the players' union have negotiated an arbitration procedure for settling salary disputes. The player and the team go before a neutral arbitrator with their final salary proposals, and both—with the player usually represented by an agent—argue the player's worth. The arbitrator ends the dispute by selecting one figure or the other.

Almon wanted $340,000 for 1982; the White Sox made a counter offer of $220,000. The arbitrator settled on the team's figure, and the matter was put to rest, but not for long. A couple of months later, *Sports Illustrated* reported some of the arguments made during the hearing, which is supposed to be private. The White Sox officials were said to have charged that Almon "lacked leadership qualities, tended to choke in the field, was inexperienced, hadn't made the All-Star team, and had batted .158 during a particular thirteen-game stretch."

Almon wasn't surprised by what he read. He had attended the hearings himself, which perhaps had been a mistake since such business meetings can sometimes get nasty. What troubled him was knowing that the arguments were supposed to be secret, and seeing them in print; he wondered why someone had let them out. "What bothers me is how the front office is looking at me now," he said at the time. "I mean, they won the hearing. Are they still mad?"*

After patching matters up with Hemond in training camp, Almon soon focused on baseball again. He got off to another fine start, beginning on Opening Day when he collected five hits as the Sox swept a doubleheader from the Yankees. In the opener, he smashed a 425-foot triple off Goose Gossage in the twelfth inning and came in to score the winning run. The next afternoon, Almon went two for three and stole a base against the Red Sox in Fenway Park. His batting average settled at around .333 for the next six weeks.

Then Almon slumped. Over the next six weeks, his average slid to .272 and he had his usual problems with errors. But Almon probably would have been given time to work out the slump had it not been for a nationally televised game against the Milwaukee Brewers on July 5. The White Sox were terrible that evening as they lost 8–4 and made seven errors. Almon was charged with two of the errors, and his play was ridiculed by the announcer, ABC's Al Michaels, who suggested that no respectable major league shortstop should make so many errors.

Almon's season might as well have ended that night. He was replaced at shortstop by Vance Law, who had been playing third base, and Aurelio Rodriguez was installed at third. Almon's batting average continued to drop, and he ended the year at .256.

---

* *Providence Journal,* February 18, 1982.

Why Almon's season fell apart isn't entirely clear. The TV game, according to some reports, brought a swift reaction from Eddie Einhorn, Chicago's owner, who ordered the benching of Almon and Ron LeFlore, and fired Ron Schueler, the team's pitching coach. Some, including Almon, wondered whether bad feelings from the arbitration case played a part in Einhorn's reaction.

Manager LaRussa insisted that no one told him who to bench and said he had been trying to get Law and Rodriguez into the lineup for weeks. He expressed regret about what happened and praised Almon as one of the most competitive players on the Sox. "It was the toughest problem I had to face all summer," he said.

Certainly Almon's errors played a part. But errors—like many baseball statistics—are open to many interpretations, and Almon had always been an erratic fielder. His errors had been excused by teams, including the White Sox, that were otherwise happy with his play, and he has often pointed out that he covers more ground than many shortstops. (He led the National League in total chances in 1977, and he and Tony Bernazard were leading the league in double plays when he was benched in 1982.) Since his range is good, Almon gets to many more balls and, as a result, has more opportunities to make errors.

"I started out as a better than average fielder," Almon says. "But what happened was that, in the beginning of my career, I had good range and I had a lot of total chances but I made a lot of errors. As far as I was concerned, the bottom line was total chances. In baseball, unfortunately, people just harp on errors and they don't really consider the situation or consider the total chances."

The focus on his errors hurt. "People just complained so

much about errors. It was pounded and pounded at me. At times, I became just afraid to make an error instead of being aggressive. It affected me," he says.

He admits that there were times when he would hope a ball would be hit to someone else—a terrible feeling to have and one that only produces more mistakes. "A tentative defensive player is as bad as a defensive hitter," he says. "It just can't be done."

In the fall of 1982, Almon again exercised his option to become a free agent. He was chosen in the draft by three teams —the New York Yankees, Cleveland Indians, and Pittsburgh Pirates—and, under baseball rules, he was then allowed to negotiate with anyone. (Only players chosen by at least four teams must sign with one of the teams that draft them.) He signed a one-year agreement with Oakland, for terms that weren't disclosed.

So far, it has been a good move for him. Oakland never got into the 1983 pennant race—the White Sox coasted to victory in the American League's Western Division with Jerry Dybzinski and Vance Law sharing the playing time at short—but Almon turned in a fine year. He led the team in batting for most of the summer and played in 143 games, his highest total since his rookie year. He drove in 63 runs, which was also a career high, and stole 26 bases. After a late season slump, he finished with a .266 batting average.

He also continued to work on his defense. He made 20 errors during the year, but his play in the outfield improved as the season progressed, and Boros said that his future in the big leagues might be as an outfielder as well as an infielder. "That's why we've been working hard with him on the defensive part of the game—not just the physical skills but the mental approach to it as well," Boros says. "That's the big hurdle he has to cross." With a young team and a fine outfield, though, Oakland is unlikely to make room in its starting lineup next season for Almon.

Bill Almon remembers that, as a youngster growing up in Rhode Island, "I was like any other American boy. I always had the dream of being a big league ballplayer." Few American boys, of course, realize that dream. Only six hundred fifty players are in the big leagues at any one time, and, by any standard, they have reached the pinnacle of their profession. They have survived years of intense competition and a long and difficult winnowing-out process.

Yet Almon, reflecting on his ten seasons of professional baseball, can look back to just three of them with a feeling of satisfaction: his rookie season in San Diego, his season as the starting shortstop for Chicago, and this past season in Oakland. Those were the years, he believes, when he was given a fair chance to show what he could do, and those were the years when he performed up to his capabilities.

As for the remaining years, Almon is not bitter. He has enjoyed playing baseball, made good friends, and made a very good living. He has lived the life that millions of others can only dream about, and he has become used to the fact that he has to go out each season and earn his job all over again.

Yet there is something a little unfair about what has happened to Bill Almon, in his roller-coaster career in baseball. It is hard to imagine any other career or profession in which someone with such highly developed skills would not be given the opportunity to use them every day. No doctor or lawyer or teacher or carpenter—at least none at the peak of a career—is denied the chance to work at what he or she does best. Almon is denied that opportunity every time he finds himself entering a game in the late innings, or getting only an occasional chance to pinch hit, or just sitting on the bench. That, for him, is by far the hardest part. "You don't," he says, "always get an opportunity to do what you love to do."

# 6 Stardom: *Steve Kemp of the New York Yankees*

If money could buy happiness, Steve Kemp would be a happy man. He has a gorgeous new home in the woods of New Jersey, a California beachfront house with a hot tub, a condominium on the water in Hawaii, fancy cars, plenty of clothes, and a fat bank account. Not bad for a guy approaching thirty.

Fulfilling a childhood dream, Kemp has made his money as a baseball star. Baseball came easily to him, and he became a successful major leaguer soon after turning professional. Now, he has a guaranteed multi-million dollar contract with the New York Yankees. He will be paid for the next six years whether he plays or not.

Kemp also enjoys the perks of stardom—the pleasure of seeing his picture on the cover of magazines, the acclaim from fans, the satisfaction of knowing that he is among the best. Blessed with exceptional talent and some good luck, he climbed rapidly to the top in a tough and competitive sport. He is convinced that he has the talent to stay on top. But these days he sometimes wonders whether his luck is running out.

He signed with the Yankees in late 1982 and looked forward

to a season that many thought would end in the World Series. Instead, 1983 turned out to be his unhappiest summer in baseball.

Kemp lost the confidence of his manager and struggled to hold onto a starting job. His season ended, not with the heady excitement of the playoffs or World Series, but with a scary eye injury.

Several months later, away from the turmoil of Yankee Stadium, Kemp tries to relax. He putters around his new house, plans a winter vacation in Hawaii, and ponders the season to come. His financial future may be secure. His future in baseball is not.

Steve Kemp turned to sports early on. Playing baseball offered a chance to escape poverty and a troubled family life.

Kemp grew up poor—not ghetto-poor, but in the rough sections of Highland Park, California, a suburb of Los Angeles. His parents divorced when he was seven. He still feels deeply that his father—who moved away from the area and lost touch with Steve and his younger brother, Ron—abandoned the family. "He was never really interested in what was going on," Kemp says. "He never sent my brother or myself any type of birthday cards or anything, and then when I was playing in the college World Series he read my name in the paper and looked me up. Now that I've been in pro ball, he looks me up every once in a while."

Before the divorce, Steve had been close to his father. His mother, Joyce Meadows, who remarried, says Steve rarely lets his emotions about the breakup surface. But shortly before his twelfth birthday, when his mother and stepfather were about to take the family on vacation, Kemp's feelings did show. His mother remembers that "Steve didn't really want to go because it was close to his birthday, and he was looking forward to a birthday card from his father. He was afraid he'd miss it if we went to the cabin.

"He went along with us, but he kept waiting and waiting for that card, but it never came. . . . That crushed Steve."*

Not all the memories are painful. Kemp fondly recalls an uncle who bought him his first baseball bat. He remembers a grade school teacher who taught him sportsmanship. And, he says, his mother supported him in everything he did.

He got a baseball glove at age four or five, a right-handed mitt that he promptly forced onto his left hand. "That's when they first found out that I was lefty," he says. Once that was settled, the game became easy for him.

He remembers only one frustration as a young player, and that had nothing to do with ability. He was turned away from Little League because he was too young. "I knew at the time that I was as good as these guys playing. It really broke my heart that I wasn't able to play."

When Kemp did play in organized leagues, he excelled. His family moved to Arcadia, a nicer town with a lively baseball program, and his Pony League team was so good that it went all the way to a Pony League World Series in Pennsylvania, where he set a couple of series records. When he looked them up in a record book, he spotted the names of several other young record-holders who had gone on to the big leagues. It was then that he first told himself, "I'm going to become a major league baseball player when I get older." He was fourteen.

Kemp was a natural, and not just at baseball. He picked up a tennis racket one day and instantly became a good player. "In high school," he says, "I used to pole vault though nobody ever

---

* This account of Kemp's childhood is drawn from a story in the *Detroit Free Press,* June 10, 1979. Kemp declined to answer further questions about his family.

taught me how." He has never taken a golf lesson, but his score is usually in the low 80s.

There seemed no limit to how far he could go. A sixth grade teacher, Mrs. Jamile, wrote in his autograph book: "This has been some year for me looking at your mischievous smile every morning. . . . I know you will lead a happy and successful life. . . . I hope to read about you in the sports section of the papers in a few years."

His father was not around anymore to cheer him on. But the applause was building for young Steve Kemp.

Spotting baseball talent early is an inexact science—Kemp's career proves that. A star in high school, he was passed over by every team in the draft held after his senior year. The scouts were apparently put off by his size—he was only 5 feet 9 inches and 150 pounds—and by the fact that he hadn't gotten along well with his high school coach.

Fortunately, a coach from the University of Southern California saw him play in a high school all-star game and suggested that he attend USC. There was just one catch—no scholarships were available.

Kemp's stepfather agreed to pay his way. Then Kemp told the coach, "I'll go, but under one condition—that if I prove myself, you'll give me some type of scholarship next year." USC agreed.

That proved to be a good deal for Kemp and USC. He won a scholarship after his freshman year, and as a sophomore he hit .351 and led the Trojans to the NCAA championship. In his junior year, he set a USC batting record by hitting .435. Coach Rod Dedeaux, who has trained dozens of collegians who became major leaguers, called him one of the best hitters he had ever seen.

Kemp played baseball for the United States in the Pan American Games in the fall of 1975 and became available for the major league draft in January 1976. This time, there was no way he would be passed over.

The Detroit Tigers made Kemp the number one selection in the draft and predicted that he soon would be playing in the majors. They gave him a big league contract—meaning that if he didn't make the majors in three years, any other team could claim him—and a bonus of about $50,000. It was a sweet moment. "My biggest achievement in baseball," he says, "is going from not being drafted out of high school to being the number one draft pick in the nation after I'd gone to college."

Being the top pick puts pressure on some players, especially those who are rushed to the majors. But Kemp feels it helped his career because of the attention he got from coaches, managers, and the Tigers' top brass. He could relax, knowing they had confidence in him. "I could have done badly, and they were going to still keep playing me, working with me, and trying to teach me," he says.

That spring he was assigned to Montgomery of the Class AA Southern League. He struggled for a few weeks—the bus rides, he says, were tiring and took time to get used to—but soon he improved to the point where he was named the league's player of the month in June. He had lifted his batting average to .289 when he was promoted to Detroit's top farm club, Evansville of the Class AAA American Association.

There he blossomed. He batted .386 with 11 home runs and 38 RBIs in 52 games in July and August. It seemed that as the quality of play improved, so did Kemp's performance. "In Triple A," he says, "the hitting was a little easier, because the pitchers had better control and were usually around the plate.

In Double A, you had guys who threw hard and didn't know where the ball was going. I was not as disciplined a hitter as I am now, and I would swing at a lot of bad pitches just because I knew they were throwing fastballs." The Tigers were impressed; they told him he would be coming to Detroit on September 1.

His progress was derailed slightly, however, when in his second-to-last game in Evanston, he tore ligaments in his ankle sliding hard into second base. Instead of going to the big leagues, he spent the next few weeks visiting doctors. Surgery was performed on the ankle, and rehabilitating it took most of the winter.

Although his ankle wasn't fully healed when he arrived for spring training in 1977, Kemp won the starting left field job with Detroit. His hustle and desire were evident, and Manager Ralph Houk was soon predicting great things for him. The ex-Yankee skipper compared his young outfielder to former New York stars Mickey Mantle and Bobby Murcer.

Houk was the ideal manager for Kemp, who is much happier when he knows that his managers and coaches are behind him. "Ralph Houk was by far the best manager I ever played for. He always instilled so much confidence in me," Kemp says. "As a rookie, it was unbelievable for me to play from the start."

At bat, Kemp managed to hold his own against big league pitching. His batting style was unorthodox—he waved his bat slightly as the pitcher wound up—but Houk and his coaches left him alone, and their confidence paid off. Kemp batted .257, hit 18 home runs, and drove in 88 runs. His batting average was a disappointment, but, overall, he was pleased. "I was never worried about my hitting because everything just came naturally," he says. "I knew I could hit, and I didn't want to change."

Yet Kemp's memories of his first summer in Detroit are not all happy. He was learning a new position, having difficulty with the fans, and experiencing personal problems.

Kemp had played center field in high school and college, but was switched to left field in the minors because coaches felt he didn't have the speed for center. He found left field a harder position. "When you play center, the ball comes at you straight. When you play left or right, the ball's hooking or it's tailing away," he says. During batting practice, Kemp would hustle out to left field and take as many fly balls as possible, trying to develop the good instincts that an outfielder needs. "It's been something that I've worked on and worked on, and I feel I do an adequate job," he says now.

He was rarely graceful, though, and his errors in the field embarrassed him, especially during his rookie year. He thinks his shortcomings in the outfield made it hard for him to win the hearts of Tiger fans. "I didn't realize it, but in the major leagues, for the fans, baseball is really based around defense," he says. "You will see players get more standing ovations for defensive plays than for offensive things they do. The fans appreciate a great defensive play."

His problems with the fans had other roots, too. In his first season, Kemp replaced longtime Tiger favorite Willie Horton in left field. Horton, who was traded early in the season, was gracious; when he left, he even had Kemp autograph a ball for his daughter. But the newcomer was sometimes greeted by chants of "We want Willie" when he trotted out to left field.

"It was not easy," Kemp remembers, "because I took over for someone who was a hero. I was young, and I couldn't understand why people were booing me. I was not happy."

Finally, Kemp's marriage was falling apart. He had wed Leanne Weitzmann in September 1976, but his promotion to the majors had strained their relationship. Among other things, she wanted a career of her own. They separated, then divorced.

Kemp's first summer in Detroit set the tone for the years to come. On the field, especially at bat, Kemp's play improved. His relations with the Tiger fans and owners did not.

In his second season, for example, Kemp showed no sign of a sophomore jinx. He hit 15 home runs, drove in 79 runs, and raised his average to .277. By the end of 1979, his third summer in Detroit, he had emerged as one of the most productive hitters in the American League. That season he hit 26 home runs, knocked in 105 runs, and batted .318, eighth best in the league. He made the All-Star team and was elected the Tiger of the Year by Detroit's baseball writers.

At about that time, Kemp was beginning to clash with the Tiger owners over his contract. The issue involved money, but went beyond it, too. The disputes reflected Kemp's feeling that he wasn't appreciated in Detroit.

Certainly he didn't need more money. Kemp invested his money carefully, and, while he enjoyed the good life, he lived within his means. Even before the salary disputes, he was doing well enough to afford a $40,000 Porsche and a beautiful home nestled between the mountains and the Pacific in Laguna Niguel, California, down the coast from Los Angeles.

But Kemp was nagged by a feeling that he was underpaid, compared with his teammates and other players. Highly touted draft picks like Kirk Gibson and Rick Leach, for instance, got bigger signing bonuses from Detroit than he had. That, he thought, wasn't fair.

The issue first surfaced in 1980. Kemp had played the previous season without a contract, and the Tigers had given him a small raise. (He won't talk specifics, so not all the salary figures are known.) For 1980, Kemp wanted to be paid $210,000; the Tigers proposed $150,000. Their disagreement simmered all winter, creating bad feelings on both sides. The Tigers complained that Kemp wouldn't join their publicity tour of Michigan, hinting that he preferred to stay home in balmy southern California. Kemp was upset when the team wouldn't fly him to Detroit to accept his Tiger of the Year Award from the writers. Ultimately, the dispute was settled by arbitration. Kemp got his $210,000, but the ill will persisted, even after he had another fine season in Detroit.

The salary fight was replayed the next winter. This time the stakes were higher: Kemp wanted $600,000; Detroit proposed $360,000. But the result was the same: Kemp won. He could command that salary because he had become one of baseball's top hitters. A chart produced by Kemp and his agent, Richard Moss, showed that he placed twelfth among all major leaguers in runs produced (RBIs plus runs scored, minus homers) in his four years in the majors. Of the players ahead of him on the list, only two—Ken Singleton and Steve Garvey—were paid less than what the Tigers offered, while seven others earned $800,000 a year or more. Such arguments persuaded the arbitrator, and Kemp felt, above all, that he had proved his point. "Money was not the big factor for me. The principle of knowing what I'm worth was," he says.

Tiger fans didn't see it that way. Many could not bring themselves to root for a rich young man who squabbled over money, drove a foreign car, and lived in California. Some felt Kemp was greedy and unappreciative of the wealth baseball had brought him.

"It was hard for them because Detroit was going through some difficult times," Kemp says. "They couldn't understand how a guy playing baseball—something they would love to do—could be making that kind of money. . . . I put up with a lot of crap."

Kemp was not even the best-paid Tiger—catcher Lance Parrish made more—but to fans in Detroit he became a symbol of the spoiled young stars. They became unforgiving of his bad nights. While he had a few loyalists who brought banners to the ballpark and wrote encouraging letters, they were outnumbered by the detractors. Especially if he had struck out or left a runner on base in his previous at-bat, the boos drowned out the cheers when he approached the plate. One night in June 1981, he struck out three times and was booed mercilessly.

"I just don't think I'll ever forget what happened last night," he said the next day. "If they expected me to always be a hero, they're out of their minds. . . . I don't understand them. Maybe they're hoping to run me out of here."

He felt abandoned by the team management and unwanted by the fans. "At the age of twenty-six, here I am—I should be having fun, that's what the game's for, to enjoy. I should be able to look forward to coming to the ballpark. And it's not that way."* He let it be known that he wanted to leave Detroit.

The Tigers were happy to oblige. They realized that they would probably lose Kemp, and get nothing in return, when he became eligible for free agency at the end of 1982. In November 1981, Detroit traded him to the Chicago White Sox for outfielder Chet Lemon.

The deal worked out reasonably well for everyone. Kemp had a good season in Chicago (.286, 19 HRs, 98 RBIs), Lemon did fairly well in Detroit, and both teams were happy. The White

---

* *Detroit News,* June 3, 1981.

Sox said they wanted to sign Kemp to a long-term contract at the end of the year but never made a serious offer. "I enjoyed playing in Chicago, and I would have liked to have stayed there," he says. "Things just didn't work out." So he entered the open market.

While Kemp was certainly well-paid in Detroit and Chicago, he owes his current good fortune to the wealthy owner of the New York Yankees, George M. Steinbrenner III. Kemp announced his decision to sign with New York at baseball's winter meetings in Hawaii in December 1982, and perhaps because there were already a half-dozen or so millionaires on the Yankees, his contract did not attract much notice. Nevertheless, the story of how Kemp came to the Yankees is interesting, both for what it shows about baseball salaries and for what it says about how valuable a player Kemp had become in just six years.

Just a decade earlier, Willie Mays, perhaps the greatest ballplayer in modern times, became the highest paid player in New York baseball history. His salary: $165,000 a year. Slugger Dick Allen, the American League's most valuable player in 1972, became the first player ever to earn $250,000 in one year.

Free agency—the system in which a player is free to sell his services to any team after a certain number of years—has changed all that. Now teams must compete in the marketplace for top players who can command the salaries they want.

Kemp's experience was typical. While he was one of forty-one free agents available in the fall of 1982, only a handful—Kemp, Don Baylor, Steve Garvey, and Floyd Bannister—were premium performers. To wealthy owners like Steinbrenner, California's Gene Autry, and Atlanta's Ted Turner, capturing the top free agents goes beyond improving their teams; it is a matter of personal pride as well. Steinbrenner especially has built his teams with expensive free agents such as Catfish Hunter, Reggie Jackson, and Dave Winfield.

Kemp is not a superstar in the class of Winfield or Jackson. He has never been an MVP or a league leader in home runs or runs batted in. His fielding is no better than average. He is, however, a proven hitter, and at the time he was deemed one of the finest young players in the game. Excluding 1981, the season interrupted by a players' strike, Kemp had averaged 19 home runs and 94 runs batted in a year during his career. His lifetime batting average was .285. Nine teams selected him during the free agent draft in November; Baltimore, Philadelphia, and the White Sox pursued him seriously.

Steinbrenner made it clear that he wanted Kemp—and not just because of his statistics. Kemp had earned a reputation as a hard-working, aggressive ballplayer. Kemp runs out ground balls at top speed and usually gets his uniform dirty by the end of a game. In the outfield, he slams into fences in pursuit of fly balls with alarming frequency. Steinbrenner was willing to part with his millions to bring that style of play to the Yankees. "I'm a discipline guy. I like hustle," Steinbrenner said then. "Steve is the supreme hustler. He'll turn New York on."

The Yankee owner also made a personal appeal to Kemp—taking him to lunch, showing him around New York, suggesting places for him to live in New Jersey. Kemp, who had felt undervalued by owners for most of his career, appreciated the personal touch. "George was just super to me," he says. "That's one reason I decided to come here."

The contract helped, too. Kemp signed a five-year deal worth $5.45 million in salaries, bonuses, performance incentives, and long-term payments. The entire contract, with the exception of the performance bonuses, is guaranteed—meaning he will be paid whether he plays or not.

From his experience in Detroit, Kemp understands that big salaries can stir resentment among fans. But he says he wasn't surprised by the contract. "I felt that was what I deserved."

Kemp says a sorting-out process occurs—in high school, college, the minor leagues, and even the majors—and only those with the skill and determination to succeed reach the top. As for those who don't make it, Kemp says, "They didn't continue to work at it. It didn't hold their interest. They had better things to do. I didn't. I enjoyed playing baseball, and I worked at it, and it's paid off."

While some critics say that long-term contracts remove the incentive for players to improve, Kemp scoffs at the notion. Those who know him agree; they say he is driven to excel in baseball by forces other than money.

"To me, the money is all secondary," he insists. "I really don't think about the contract. I just want to go out and do well. That's what's important to me."

While his negotiations with the Yankees were friendly, they raised the same issues as did his salary squabbles in Detroit. The money in his new contract was important, not for what it could buy, but as a symbol of his worth. He had entered free agency, in fact, with the declaration that he would not sign for any less than his friend and former teammate, Jason Thompson, who had just signed a five-year, $5.25 million deal with Pittsburgh. Even as an established star, Steve Kemp needed to know that he was appreciated. George Steinbrenner filled that need, and he still does; the two men continue to get along well.

Not long after becoming a Yankee, though, Kemp found that

it was harder to please the man with day-to-day command of the team—his volatile manager, Billy Martin.

Kemp felt terrific when he reported to the Yankees' spring training base in Fort Lauderdale. He was looking forward to playing in Yankee Stadium, with its great tradition and the short right field fence that delights left-handed sluggers.

Kemp, Winfield, and Baylor were being hailed as the latest edition of Murderer's Row—a term used as far back as the 1920s to describe Yankee sluggers. In one oft-quoted remark, Kemp said he saw no reason why the three of them couldn't drive in more than 300 runs—a reasonable assumption since they had knocked in 297 the year before.

In the exhibition season, Kemp led the team with a .450 batting average, 4 homers, and 18 RBIs. Winfield and Baylor also excelled as the Yankees rolled up a 16–8 record, their best exhibition performance since 1970.

Kemp's surge carried over into the season. He had a home run on Opening Day, and went 6 for 18 with two homers, a triple, a double, and four RBIs in the Yankees' first four games.

Then, in a game on April 10 in Toronto, he went chasing after a pop fly and instead collided with two teammates, Willie Randolph and Jerry Mumphrey. Kemp dropped the ball for an error that led to a five-run Toronto rally. That was bad enough, but Kemp's right shoulder became so stiff after the game that he feared serious damage. Doctors found a chipped bone and told him no operation was needed. But they said that he might be in pain for the rest of the year.

After sitting out two games, Kemp was back. "I figured, I'm getting paid to play, I'm going to play," he says. "I had to do what I thought was right."

His performance suffered. He hit .220 in the next 13 games and managed just one home run. He insisted at the time that the shoulder wasn't bothering him: "I could easily say 'my shoulder's sore and that's why I'm not swinging the bat good.' But that has nothing to do with it."*

Kemp wasn't being honest. Now he says the shoulder was "tight as a drum" for a couple of months, and he should have rested it. It was his worst injury since reaching the major leagues, but coming as it did—early in the season, when he was hot—he didn't want to sit down. He says the decision to keep playing was his alone. "That was just the way I wanted to be," he says. "I played for two months with it bad, and I never should have. It was my decision to make, and I screwed up. But if I had to do it over again, I would do it again. I would play."

The Yankees, meanwhile, started slowly. They returned from a West Coast trip in late May with a 20–21 record and the pressure building on Martin, who had been fired twice before by Steinbrenner. Looking to his talent-laden bench, he decided to make use of more players.

In one stretch, Martin used eleven different lineups in eleven days, trying to get the most out of his manpower. He shuffled Kemp and Baylor, the free agent prizes, in and out of the lineup to make room for each other and for subs like Oscar Gamble and Lou Piniella. There was no clear pattern to the lineup changes, and Martin wasn't doing much explaining.

"If some guys are unhappy, that's their problem," Martin said. "I'm here to win, and I'll go about that the way I know how." Neither Baylor nor Kemp liked the system.

Kemp, mired in the deepest slump of his career, felt he was

---

* *Hartford Courant,* April 30, 1983.

in no position to gripe. However, Martin's platoon system was instituted just when Kemp most needed the manager's support, and in retrospect he thinks that the uncertainty over his role made matters worse. "If I had Billy's approval, then I could just go out and play my game," Kemp says. "If somebody just lets me play, I can produce. But when somebody's looking over me day to day and saying, 'If you don't get a hit today, you're out tomorrow, and then you might be in there two or three days from now'—well, I can't play like that."

The pain in his shoulder had subsided, but the injury, coupled with his desire to please Martin, had contributed to a mental problem. Kemp began to press too hard.

"I wanted to win his confidence. By doing that, then I could relax," he says. "But to win his confidence, I had to try to do more than I was probably capable of doing—trying to hit a home run every at-bat instead of just taking my hits or walks or whatever. It really screwed me up."

In late June, the Yankees went to Boston for a three-game series against the Red Sox. Kemp sat out the first game, except to pinch hit and ground into a double play. New York lost, 5–4, and he said afterward, "My head was all jumbled. There was so much extra pressure. Not just to play good baseball, but to impress him [Martin]."*

Sensing that Kemp needed a boost, Martin came to him before the next day's game to say that, from then on, he would be the everyday right fielder. It was a risk for the embattled manager, since Kemp was hitting just .250 and producing few runs.

Kemp responded immediately. That day, he drove in three runs with a homer, a double, and a single. He hit the ball well

---

* *Hartford Courant,* June 26, 1983.

over the next two weeks, going 8 for 18 when he played. (Martin sat him down for a couple of days.) By the All-Star break, Kemp had raised his average to .272 and was second on the team to Winfield in RBIs with 39. "I thought, okay, I'm on my way now," he says.

But Kemp, as it turned out, was having a season much like the Yankee team—each time the team looked as if it had shed its losing ways and began to make a run for the pennant, it slipped again. Kemp could not keep his batting streak going.

"I came back from the All-Star break, and I went 0 for 17, but with just one strikeout. So I was hitting the ball, but I wasn't getting any hits," he says. "I got benched. Then I started getting platooned, and everything just snowballed to make it a bad year."

Martin went back on his promise. He was unwilling to be patient with the slumping Kemp, especially given the talent on the team. Don Mattingly, a hot-hitting rookie, was challenging for the right field job.

"I can't get totally upset with Billy," Kemp says. "You figure that bench is a temptation. His job's in jeopardy, so he's going to put somebody else out there."

Even if Martin's lineup juggling makes some sense, however, the way he treated the unhappy players that his system created does not. Kemp doesn't want to blame his problems on someone else, but it seems as if he was badly mishandled by Martin. This is especially so because Kemp requires more support—a little more fathering, perhaps—than many other players.

"Confidence is probably the most important thing in this game," Kemp says, "and that's why a manager is so important to a player. Because if a manager has no confidence in a player, then it's easy for a player to lose confidence in himself."

In Kemp's scheme of things, it's essential for him to have a good working relationship with his manager. "I don't have to have dinner with them, or go out and have a drink with them, or anything like that. I don't need them to pat me on the ass. I just like to know that I can go in and talk. I was that way with Ralph [Houk] and I was that way with Sparky [Anderson] and I was that way with [Tony] LaRussa."

Kemp and LaRussa, for example, had several loud arguments over Kemp's position in the batting order. Kemp now calls them "great conversations."

"You tell him what you feel, and he can tell you what he feels. What it basically comes down to is . . . he's going to make the final decision because he's the manager. But at least he knows where you're coming from, and you know why he's doing certain things. If one game I'm hitting third and the next game I'm hitting eighth, I want to know why.

"But Billy doesn't believe in talking. He doesn't have to explain anything to anybody. That's his way."

Martin also doesn't believe that a player should publicly question or criticize a manager. So when Kemp told a couple of reporters that he had a "communications problem" with Martin and missed the rapport he'd had with Houk and Anderson, things only got worse. After that, Kemp recalls, Martin "came up to me and patted me on the back and he goes, 'There. How's that for communication?' Then he said, sarcastically, 'You get a hit tonight or you're not in there tomorrow.' "

That's not a good way to motivate a player, but somehow Kemp hit a home run off Dan Petry to put the Yanks ahead in a close game. "While I was rounding the bases, I was saying to myself, all right, I get to play tomorrow," he says. "It wasn't any big deal about putting us ahead—which is not the way it should be."

By the end of the summer, it sometimes seemed as if Martin was so upset with Kemp that he was programming him to fail. On a trip to the West Coast, Kemp sat out a series of games against right-handed pitchers because the manager wanted to get Mattingly into the lineup. The left-handed Kemp's next chance to start a game came against Pete Vukovich, a tough right-hander, in Milwaukee. He went 0 for 2, with a couple of walks, and found himself back on the bench the next day even though the Brewers were using a righty. "The reporters and everybody said they couldn't understand it," Kemp says.

The Milwaukee game turned out to be Kemp's last of 1983. Two days later, on September 8, before the final game of the series, he strolled out toward left field during batting practice, chatting with a teammate and preparing to take some fungos. He turned his back to the plate, where teammate Omar Moreno was hitting.

"The batting practice pitcher threw the ball, and the ball was hit. Someone yelled 'heads up' and I turned around and it smacked me right in the eye," Kemp says.

The ball was hit solidly, and Kemp was about 150 feet from the plate in short left field. "It was a line drive," he says. "It wasn't a Dave Winfield line drive—fortunately—or it would have killed me.

"I remember hitting the ground, and I was spitting blood all over the place. Broken teeth were in my mouth. I thought, 'Oh man, I've gotta just pass out.' Then I thought, 'No, I better not, because I've heard of people passing out and never regaining consciousness.' Then I just tried to keep my sense of humor because I was in pain."

His teammates and a trainer bent over him, and eventually several of them carried a bloodied Kemp on a stretcher from the field to a waiting ambulance. On the way to the hospital, he recalls hearing that his blood pressure was something like 210 over 120. He said, "Jesus Christ, are my veins going to break or what?"

The scariest moment came when he arrived at the hospital. A doctor or nurse covered his good eye and asked, "Can you see how many fingers I have up?"

"I can't see anything," Kemp replied. "All I can do is tell if the light's on."

Suddenly, nothing else—not his $5.45 million contract, not his low batting average, not even his troubles with Billy Martin—seemed to matter anymore.

On a rainy, dreary afternoon in mid-November, Steve Kemp sits in the dining room of his home in northern New Jersey and thinks about the baseball season just past and the one ahead. He is in a reasonably good mood; he still can't see well out of his right eye, but his vision is improving, and so are his spirits.

Kemp and his second wife, Mary Kay, moved into this home—a contemporary wood structure with airy rooms, angular ceilings, and skylights—last spring, but they have not had a chance to furnish it completely. The dining room, for example, has a couple of couches but no table. Today the house is busy; workmen are installing an elaborate stereo system.

Despite the unfinished look, it's obvious that this is a ballplayer's house. The walls of the entryway are covered by photographs, newspaper clippings, and magazine covers of Kemp and Mary Kay, a former model. One shows Kemp on the cover of the *Sporting News* last April with the legend, "A New Cannon in New York, Steve Kemp Joins Arsenal as Yanks Stress

Power Again." Baseball bats are piled on a couch; Kemp has collected them from fellow players like Carl Yazstremski, Rod Carew, and George Brett.

Two weeks earlier, Kemp swung a bat himself for the first time since the injury in Milwaukee. He worked out in an area below Yankee Stadium with a batting practice pitcher. The results were encouraging. "I was seeing the ball pretty good," he says.

The ball that hit Kemp on the left side of his face in September fractured his cheekbone, broke a half dozen teeth, and damaged the tissue behind his left eye. For a few days, Kemp wore an eyepatch and didn't know whether he would be able to see. "I was scared," he says.

Steinbrenner, who was traveling with the team, went to the hospital with Kemp and quickly arranged to have Mary Kay brought out. Kemp had twenty stitches around the eye and surgery done on his retina before leaving the hospital a week later to return to New York. Steinbrenner provided a private jet to take him home.

Dozens of visits to doctors followed. "I've probably spent a total of twenty-five or thirty hours just in the dentist's chair," Kemp says. He saw eye doctors and bone specialists as well as dentists and the regular team physician, Dr. John Bonamo.

Kemp, who had superb vision before the injury, can read the bottom line on the eye chart again. But he says the letters are blurry, and he can't seem to get rid of some dark spots that appear in front of his eyes.

"My eyesight is nowhere near what it used to be," he says. "My vision is blurred as of right now, and I've got some areas that are darked out. It's like looking through a chain link fence."

Kemp has few good memories of his first summer in Yankee pinstripes, which he calls "by far the most difficult" of his baseball career. He finished with a .241 batting average, 12 home runs, and 49 RBIs. Being on the bench was a deeply unsettling experience. It was so hard to take, he says, that he responded to his injury by telling himself, "Maybe there was a reason for it. Maybe this pain and agony would be nothing compared to what I would have gone through the last month of the season just sitting on the bench or being platooned or playing once in a crucial situation."

He is now preparing himself, physically and mentally, for the 1984 season. He works out nearly every day on a Nautilus machine, plays racquetball and golf, and plans to do more hitting and throwing. Assuming his eye comes around, he expects to be in good physical condition for spring training.

However, as for his mental readiness, "I won't know until I get down there and see who I'm playing for," he says. "I don't think if I'm playing for Billy that I'll be real strong unless he can come up to me and say with a straight face that I'm going to be playing every day. But, whoever I'm playing for, I think that, mentally, I know what I'm up against. I'm ready for the challenge."*

It's amazing what a difference a year can make. The previous fall, Kemp was one of the most sought-after players in the game as teams competed to pay millions for his services. He had proven himself in the big leagues; his goals were ambitious. He had hoped to drive in 100 runs, make the All-Star team, and play in the World Series.

---

* During the winter of 1983, Martin was replaced by Yogi Berra as the Yankees' manager.

Now Kemp must prove himself all over again, merely to regain a starting role. He is confident that he will succeed. "I'm real optimistic that I'm going to have a good year next year," he says.

One thing is certain: if he does not succeed, it will not be for lack of trying. The danger, in fact, may be that he will begin the season with so much to prove that he will try to do too much, in an effort to forget the pain of last season in a hurry. He does not want to be remembered as the Steve Kemp of 1983. Striving for the approval that stardom brings, Kemp is determined to reach the top again.

"I don't think I'll ever be a Babe Ruth or a great, great player who will be remembered forever and ever," Kemp admits. "But, you know, there are lots of players who were great, and I don't even know their names.

"What's important to me is that the people I play with and play against respect me as a player. I would like just one thing when I leave the game—that people would say, hey, he was a hard player. That's what I want people to say about Steve Kemp."

# 7 Autumn: *Ferguson Jenkins of the Chicago Cubs*

On a chilly afternoon in April 1983, Ferguson Jenkins walks to the center of the diamond in Chicago's Wrigley Field and settles onto a familiar spot—the pitcher's mound. A new baseball season is about to start, and Jenkins is ready to begin his nineteenth year in the major leagues.

That, by itself, is quite an accomplishment. The average big league baseball player spends about five years in the majors, while a good player lasts for about ten seasons. Baseball, like most sports, is meant to be played by young men.

Yet Jenkins, who is almost forty, is neither a veteran who is over the hill nor a sentimental favorite. He is the undisputed ace of the Chicago Cubs' pitching staff. This afternoon marks the eighth time he has been chosen as the Cubs' Opening Day pitcher, and each time the reason is the same: he is the best they have.

His record in 1982 proves that. Jenkins won 14 games, more than any other Cub pitcher, and his earned run average of 3.15 was the lowest on the team and thirteenth best in the National League. He also led the Cubs in starts (34), innings pitched (217), and strikeouts (134).

Jenkins first became a star with the Cubs in the late sixties and early seventies as a young fastballer who anchored the team's pitching staff. In his early years, he was what baseball people call a thrower—a pitcher with overpowering strength and speed who does not have to worry about what the hitter can do.

As he learned his craft, his career settled into a satisfying pattern. For six seasons in a row, 1967–72, he was the Cubs' Opening Day pitcher, and each time he went on to win 20 or more games. Over the years he has started more than 550 games and pitched more than 4,000 innings, making him one of the most consistent and durable pitchers of his time.

Now, by necessity, he is a thinking pitcher. While he is nowhere near as fast as he used to be, he is able to control the ball and change speeds in ways that confuse the hitters and keep them off balance. Over and over again, baseball people describe Jenkins by using the same phrase: he knows how to pitch.

"It's not just picking the ball up and throwing it to the

catcher," Jenkins says about his style of pitching. "It's knowing what pitch you want to throw, and what pitch you want the hitter to swing at."

As he has aged, Jenkins has become part of a baseball phenomenon—he is one of a growing number of older players who continue to perform well. Noting the trend in the spring of 1983, some sportswriters call it the Golden Age of Baseball. Carl Yazstremski, forty-three, Pete Rose, forty-one, and Joe Morgan, thirty-nine, are productive hitting stars even as their careers draw to an end, while a trio of forty-four-year-old pitchers—Gaylord Perry, Phil Niekro, and Jim Kaat—are confounding skeptics who wrote them off years ago. In that crowd, Jenkins, thirty-nine, can feel like a youngster.

One reason the ballplayers are staying around longer is money. As baseball salaries have inflated, players who maintain their skills can earn more than they ever did during their prime. Jenkins took full advantage of his success in 1982 when it came time to negotiate a contract for 1983. He and his agent persuaded the Cubs to give him a two-year contract worth $1.3 million, by far the most he had ever earned. (He was paid $125,000 a year in the mid-seventies after winning 20 games for six years in a row.)

A second explanation for the aging of the big leagues is that today's players spend more time on conditioning. Jenkins runs, lifts weights, and works on his farm in the off-season, and, while his waist is thicker and his hair is thinner than it used to be, his right arm, which matters most, is in good shape. He is a happy man as he looks ahead to the new season.

"My arm has never felt better, so that's no problem," he says. "When I have a uniform on, it thinks it's twenty-five."*

---

* *Wall Street Journal,* April 4, 1983.

The lure of career milestones is also cited by older players as a reason to stay on. Jenkins feels his skills as a pitcher have never been fully appreciated, and he is approaching some career achievements that could bring him more recognition. He begins this season with 278 wins, fourth among all active pitchers, and he wants very much to win 300—an accomplishment recorded by only sixteen pitchers in baseball history.

He has another goal, too, that keeps him going. He wants to pitch in a championship playoff or World Series, something he has never done in all his years in baseball. That, however, looks like a long shot in 1983. The Cubs finished fifth last year, and they haven't enjoyed a winning season since 1972.

On Opening Day, Jenkins pitches well but loses, 3–0, to Steve Rogers and the Montreal Expos. Having played so long with poor teams, he has, unfortunately, become accustomed to losing even on his good days. He has 217 losses to go along with his 278 wins.

"I enjoy winning, but I can't win every time I go out there," he says. "So I've resigned myself to the process of adjusting to the losses. I've lost a lot of ballgames—a lot because of my own undoing and a lot because of someone else's undoing."

The Cubs, too, are used to losing, but they can afford to be more patient about it than Jenkins. The team's new owners, The Chicago Tribune Co., take a long-term view of the future as they talk about "building a new tradition."

As an older player, Jenkins may not fit into those plans. Certainly he has been a great star. But perhaps the time has come for him to look to his own future, to think about retiring from baseball and beginning something new.

No matter how long Fergie Jenkins pitches in the major leagues, one thing is certain: he is not hanging around baseball because he has nowhere else to go. For some years, he has been planning for the day he takes off the uniform for the last time.

Jenkins is a rancher. He owns eighty-five head of cattle and more than two hundred acres of grazing land in the town of Blenheim, Ontario. During the baseball season, a couple of hired hands run the farm, but come fall, Jenkins takes over. He likes supervising the harvest of feed grain, caring for the animals, and just walking the land. His wife, Katherine, and three daughters—Kimberly, fourteen, Delores, thirteen, and Kelly, six—live on the farm year-round.

"Farm life is very peaceful," Jenkins says. "It's been a very productive life for me so far, and my kids enjoy it. They've seen animals being born. They know how they're made and how they grow and live. The kids have the opportunity to grow up in a slow-moving atmosphere. They have a chance to learn something."

When Jenkins retires to Blenheim, he will be returning to an area that is not far from his boyhood home. His farm is about ten miles from Chatham, Ontario, where he was raised. The Jenkinses were one of a few black families in Chatham. His father, a native Canadian and former merchant marine, worked as a chauffeur. His mother, who lost her sight because of complications when Fergie was born, stayed at home. He was an only child.

His first sport was hockey, and he was a good skater by the time he was six. He began playing baseball and football soon afterward. "My dad was a pretty good sportsman, and he showed me a lot of things," Fergie says.

While Ferguson Jenkins Sr. had been an outfielder in the Canadian Negro Leagues, baseball was not young Fergie's best sport. His high school, in fact, had no baseball team, so Fergie played sandlot baseball in the summer and nearly every other sport in high school. "My best sport was hockey. Second was basketball, and third was baseball. I also played on the golf team and I ran track and field. I used to make all-star teams, all-city teams, whatever, in basketball and hockey and football." (After making the big leagues, Jenkins toured Canada for two winters with a Harlem Globetrotters team.)

He didn't begin pitching until he was about sixteen. "That's when a lot of scouts started noticing that I had a pretty good arm," he says. "I was able to throw the ball harder than the other kids on the team. I was able to get people out pretty easily."

Life in the country provided plenty of ways to hone his skills. "When I was a kid, I used to practice five or six hours a day—just throwing the ball at certain spots," he recalls. "I used to draw a spot on the wall or on the barn, and I used to throw rocks at it, or, if I had some old baseballs, I'd see how many times I could hit the spot.

"I used to throw at boxcars, too, as they went by. I used to be able to throw a rock at a train car and hit any part of the car I wanted to. If it had both doors open, I could throw it between the doors as the train passed."

Jenkins was urged to stick with baseball by his father, who said it was the sport where he could make the most money. The big league scouts agreed. Soon after graduating from high school in 1962, Fergie signed as a free agent with the Phillies. They gave him a $7,000 bonus.

Jenkins spent three years in the minor leagues, pitching in Miami, Buffalo, Chattanooga, and Little Rock, and doing well at each stop. In 1964, for example, he struck out 149 batters in 139 innings while pitching for Chattanooga of the Southern League, an AA league.

He was called up as a relief pitcher by the Phillies in 1965.

His first game as a big leaguer was memorable. Coming in to relieve Jim Bunning in the eighth inning with the score tied and two men on, he ended the threat by striking out Dick Groat, the first man up. Then he pitched four scoreless innings as the game stretched into the twelfth to pick up his first win. He made six more appearances, all in relief, before being dealt to the Cubs the next spring. Chicago sent pitchers Larry Jackson and Bob Buhl to Philadelphia in exchange for Jenkins, John Herrnstein, and outfielder Adolpho Phillips. Phillips was seen as the key man in the deal because the Cubs needed a center fielder, but by 1972 Jenkins was the only one of the players left in the big leagues.

Jenkins says that even he did not recognize his own potential back then. In retrospect he says he did not know much about pitching. "When I was with the Phillies, I was only twenty-one years old. I was more a thrower than anything else." His fastball was in the 90 mph range. "I had a good breaking ball, but I was noted for my fastball. I had the arm to be overpowering." Big—6 feet 5 inches, 210 pounds—and strong, Jenkins threw with a loose, easy motion.

Unlike some successful young pitchers, Jenkins began to study the game—he found that big league pitchers and pitching coaches were willing to tutor him and share their secrets. During his stint with the Phils, for example, pitching coach Cal McLish taught Jenkins how to throw the slider, which later became his bread-and-butter pitch. Robin Roberts, who joined the Cubs in the final year of his career, showed Jenkins different grips to use on breaking pitches. Cub Coach Joe Becker prodded him to work harder at the game and taught him a more compact windup.

"I was just learning from day to day," Jenkins says. "I used to watch and study the other right-handed pitchers on the staff to see what they threw, how they threw, how they set hitters up. I basically learned how to pitch from watching other people perform, and then I learned to execute it myself."

In 1966, his first full major league season, Jenkins was one of the few bright spots on a hapless Cub team that lost 103 games to finish last in the National League. Jenkins appeared in 60 games, posting a 6–8 record and a respectable 3.31 earned run average. He began the season in the bullpen, but Manager Leo Durocher moved him into the starting rotation midway through the summer.

The twenty-three-year-old Jenkins was the Cubs' Opening Day starter the next spring, and he got the team off to a good start with a win over his old team, the Phillies. Though it was only his first full season as a starter in the big leagues, Jenkins proved to be durable and effective. He finished with a won-lost mark of 20–13, a 2.80 ERA, and 236 strikeouts. He also led the league in complete games with 20.

One highlight of his season was his first appearance in an All-Star game. In a superbly pitched fifteen-inning game that the National League won, 2–1, Jenkins was the most spectacular of the pitchers. He worked the fourth, fifth, and sixth innings, striking out Mickey Mantle, Rod Carew, Harmon Killebrew, Tony Oliva, Tony Conigliaro, and Jim Fregosi to tie an All-Star record with six K's.

With Jenkins leading the pitchers, and veterans Ernie Banks, Ron Santo, and Billy Williams providing the offense, Chicago surged to a surprising third place finish. Their 87–74 record was the best by any Cub team since 1946.

The following season, Jenkins and the Cubs continued to win. Even considering that 1968 was a great year for pitchers, Jenkins was impressive. He started 40 games, finished 20, and pitched 308 innings. He struck out 260 batters, second in the league to Bob Gibson, and walked only 65. He won 20 games and lost 15—five of them by 1–0 scores—and lowered his earned run average to 2.63. The Cubs, meanwhile, finished third, proving that the previous season had not been a fluke and establishing themselves as pennant contenders.

Jenkins had found he could win in the majors with his good stuff—a hard fastball and good slider. But he wanted to become a smart pitcher, too. He began to practice "situation pitching" —varying his pitches depending on the batter's abilities, the ballpark, the score of the game, the inning, and the count.

"I didn't learn to pitch in the major leagues until I'd won 20 games for the second year in a row," he says. "I learned to have a good selection of pitches—what to throw, when to throw it, and where to put them. I learned to have more confidence in each pitch I threw."

He learned not only to analyze the hitters but to analyze himself. "Every time you go and warm up in the bullpen, you're not going to have an excellent fastball or an excellent slider or a good curveball or a good changeup. So you have to pick from three or four or five pitches. It's knowing what your strengths are and what your capabilities are when you go out there."

Lee Elia, who was a teammate of Jenkins in those years and later his manager on the Cubs, says the difference between a good pitcher and a great pitcher is that a great pitcher has the ability to stretch his talent, even on bad days. "Any good pitcher —almost anybody on the major league level—is going to beat you on the day they have good stuff, or be close to beating you," Elia says. "A great pitcher can beat you on the day when he doesn't have good stuff. Right from the beginning, Fergie was a thinking pitcher. He became a great competitive pitcher because . . . he learned in a hurry."

In 1969, Jenkins and the Cubs made their strongest run at the pennant in more than two decades. They led the league by nine and a half games in mid-August, and the famed bleacher bums of Wrigley Field were going wild. Sometimes they stayed in their seats, celebrating, for more than an hour after a game ended.

The Cubs had a fine team, winning 92 games, but the summer belonged to the club called the Miracle Mets. The Cubs and the Mets—whose rivalry in the past had usually settled the question of which team would occupy the league cellar—met in September for an important three-game series, and the Mets won all three. The Cubs never recovered—a bitter disappointment, especially to the veterans on the team.

Jenkins has never forgotten. "You remember the team that gets into the World Series," Jenkins says. "You remember the Ron Swoboda catch, the Tommie Agee catch, a J. C. Martin push bunt down the first base line, or Tom Seaver in a playoff game or Jerry Koosman winning two games in the World Series. You don't remember Ron Santo hitting 29 home runs and driving in 123 runs.

"This is a thing that people just learn to go through," he continues. "You just can't play on a pennant winner every time you play. You can't get into a World Series. You have to go out there and work hard at what you do, and try to be a winner or a productive individual at your position."

The 1969 season set a pattern that was repeated over the next three years by Jenkins and the Cubs. He won his 20 games, pitched 300 or so innings, and placed among the league leaders in complete games and strikeouts. He made the All-Star team again in 1971 and 1972.

The Cubs were just as consistent—winning between 83 and

92 games, contending for the pennant through much of the summer, and each time falling short. There were numerous theories as to why they failed—some said the pitching wasn't deep enough, some faulted the manager, and many said the team became tired in the late going because it had to play all its home games during the day. The Cubs have never put lights in Wrigley Field.

Some of Jenkins' frustrations were eased when he was the overwhelming choice for the Cy Young Award in 1971, his fifth consecutive 20-game-winning season. He won 24 games while losing 13, and led the league in innings pitched (325), games started (39), complete games (30), and wins. He struck out 263 men and walked just 37. The ratio of strikeouts to walks—more than six to one—was perhaps his most eye-popping statistic.

The award gave Jenkins a rare moment in the spotlight. His skills had been largely overlooked by the national press, partly because the Cubs were never a glamour team. Even in Chicago, Jenkins had been overshadowed by longtime favorites Banks and Santo and the brash and colorful Durocher. The award helped Jenkins negotiate a salary of $125,000 a year for the next two years. That was more than any Cub had ever earned.

When Jenkins won 20 games again in 1972, he became one of only three pitchers in the last fifty years to win 20 games six seasons in a row. Robin Roberts and Warren Spahn are the others.

In 1973, Jenkins got off to a slow start and never recovered. The *Chicago Tribune* ran a banner headline blaring, "Fergie Wonders: Where Is Old Magic?" and he was quoted as saying that he was getting tired of coming out to the ballpark.

For the first time, but certainly not the last, critics wondered whether Jenkins had been overworked during the preceding years. While Jenkins had not yet turned thirty, he had generated such high expectations from his string of 20-game seasons that he was under pressure to reach that plateau each year. He found that even during years when he won 12 to 15 games—a respectable number—the reaction was that he was no longer the pitcher he used to be.

The Cubs, meanwhile, started strong and stayed in the pennant race until the second to last day of the season, when they dropped the first game of a doubleheader to their old rivals, the Mets. Jenkins started the nightcap, hoping to win his fifteenth game, finish the season at .500, and spoil the Mets' pennant chances.

The Mets scored three unearned runs in the first inning after a wild throw by Santo. Then, in the sixth, with a 3–1 count on John Milner, a blister broke on Jenkins' pitching hand. Jenkins was urged to leave the game by his teammates and by Manager Whitey Lockman, but he refused. "He had blood all over his finger," Santo said. "There was no way he could get anything on his pitches."

Jenkins walked Milner and gave up a long homer to Cleon Jones that put the game out of reach. It was the thirty-sixth homer of the year off Jenkins, and his farewell to the fans at Wrigley. The Cubs lost, 9–3, and finished out their season the next day as fewer than 2,000 fans saw them lose again to the Mets, who won the division title. Fergie ended the year with a 14–16 record and a 3.89 ERA.

Jenkins was tired of Chicago. He had never liked pitching in Wrigley Field, with its cozy dimensions, and told the club he wanted a trade, preferably to a contender. Three weeks later, he was dealt to the Texas Rangers for infielders Bill Madlock and Vic Harris.

The change of scene worked. Jenkins' first season in the American League was as good, if not better, than his Cy Young Award–winning performance in 1971. Working for Manager Billy Martin, who believes in relying on his starting pitchers, Jenkins started 41 games, finished a league-leading 29 games, and pitched 328 innings. His 25–12 record was his best ever, and he would have been the leading candidate for a second Cy Young trophy had it not been for Catfish Hunter of the Oakland A's, who led his team to the world championship with an identical 25–12 mark. Texas, meanwhile, finished second in the division—an all-too-familiar experience for Fergie.

Following that fine season, Jenkins tailed off again. Over the next three years—one in Texas and two with the Boston Red Sox—Jenkins won 39 games and lost 39. In 1977, for the first time in his career, Jenkins was removed from the starting rotation and sent to work out his problems from the bullpen. His performance showed no sign of improving, and the Red Sox, figuring he was through, sent him back to Texas after the season ended for a minor league pitcher named John Poloni.

He was thirty-four, an age when many pitchers lose their effectiveness, but he never thought of quitting. "You know as an individual when you're done, and I knew I could pitch," he says.

Back in Texas, Jenkins began the 1978 season in the bullpen as a long reliever—a thankless job usually given to a pitcher who is considered less reliable than the starters and short-relief men. But when the Rangers dropped 9 of 10 games during a spell in April, Jenkins got a chance to start against the Kansas City Royals.

It marked the start of another comeback. Fergie retired the first eighteen men he faced and, exhausted, finished with a four-hitter, a 4–1 win, and a starting job. He followed with complete games against Boston and Milwaukee, allowing one run each time, and went on to his best year since 1974.

Jenkins became the ace of the Texas staff, going 18–8 with a 3.04 ERA. His strikeout total, which had dipped, climbed back up to 157. He walked only 41 men. His goal, he said happily during that season, was now to win at least 100 games in each league and a total of 250 games. He indicated he might retire after one more season, especially if the Rangers could win their division and the pennant.

They didn't, and it turned out that Jenkins' second tour of duty in Texas would be remembered not for his comeback as a pitcher but for a shocking off-the-field event. It happened on the morning of August 25, 1980. A couple of police officers led Jenkins off the playing field before a game at Toronto's Exhibition Stadium and back to the city airport, where he was arrested and charged with illegal possession of drugs.

The circumstances surrounding the arrest are murky. His baggage, along with the bags of four other team members, had been inexplicably lost during the previous night's flight from Milwaukee. Once found, they were classified as "unaccompanied luggage" and searched by the authorities, who said they found four grams of cocaine, two grams of hashish, and two ounces of marijuana in Jenkins' bag.

His first reaction was deep embarrassment. He was not only a sports hero in his country but a recipient of the Order of Canada, an award for humanitarianism. He was nervous when he left his hotel room for the first time after the arrest, and pleasantly surprised when some youngsters still wanted his autograph.

Ahead were more serious problems. The drug charges, and a

related investigation by Baseball Commissioner Bowie Kuhn, threatened to end his career. He was scratched from his next start by the Rangers, and Kuhn tried to suspend him without pay. Jenkins fought the suspension and, with the help of the players' union, won the case. The following December he stood before a Canadian judge and pleaded guilty to the cocaine charge. Citing his record of working with numerous charitable and youth organizations in Canada, the judge dropped the other charges and agreed to erase the cocaine charge as well, provided that Jenkins continue his public service work.

Since then, Jenkins has offered conflicting accounts of his experience. Not long afterward, Jenkins seemed to admit to the charge by indicating that drug use was a casual thing among big leaguers and saying that the arrest had taught him a lesson. Later, he suggested that the entire affair had been a frame-up. Now he deflects questions about drugs.

Overshadowed by the problems with drugs were continuing difficulties on the playing field. The controversy had erupted during one of his downward slides—his record fell from 18–8 in 1978 to 16–14 in 1979 to 12–12 in 1980, the year of the arrest. His next season, which was interrupted by the players' strike, was his worst ever, as his record fell to 5–8.

Rather than hang onto the aging and expensive player, the Rangers released Jenkins. He was free to negotiate with any team, but only the Cubs and the Oakland A's expressed interest. He signed a $385,000, one-year contract with the Cubs—many thought the team had made a foolish mistake—and went on to his stellar season as the club's best pitcher in 1982.

That season began in storybook fashion as the Cubs defeated the Mets, 5–0, before a near-frozen crowd in Wrigley Field. Jenkins pitched into the seventh inning, giving up five hits, and he was greeted as a returning hero.

When reporters gathered around his old locker after the game, Jenkins cautioned them not to expect too much. "I'm not going to pitch like I did in '69," he said. "There aren't going to be a lot of complete games, and I'm not going to bowl anybody over."

Fergie had little reason to be so humble. He went on to have a season that many younger pitchers can only dream about, reaching new career milestones with almost every outing. In San Diego on May 26, Jenkins threw an 0–2 fastball past the Padres' Garry Templeton for his 3,000th strikeout. After the game, Jenkins took the ball and wrote on it, "Tempy. Thanks for 3,000. Fergie," and gave it to Templeton.

Despite his age, Jenkins finished strongly. He notched an 8–2 record in his last 12 starts, with all the wins coming against contenders. He had allowed three earned runs or fewer in 28 of his 34 starts, a record that could have easily brought him close to 20 wins.

It was, in some ways, his sweetest season. He had been told by both the Red Sox and the Rangers that he could no longer pitch, and yet somehow he struggled back to become one of the top dozen or so pitchers in the National League. He did so with a combination of guile and control, since his speed was no longer a weapon. Now Jenkins used the fastball mainly to set up his curveball and slider, plus a forkball that he used against left-handed hitters. He was capable of throwing all four pitches at varying speeds and to different spots on the plate.

"I pitch now to a zone," he explains. "I pick a box—an imaginary box—where I want to pitch a guy. Up and in, down and in, up and away, low and away. I like to pitch in. I like to throw more pitches in to make the hitter think, and to set the hitter up to go away.

"You have to think clearly when you're out there," he goes

on. "You have to make a decision, and it's got to be the right one. You have no second thoughts. If you have misgivings, you shouldn't go out there, you shouldn't put a uniform on, you shouldn't throw a certain pitch. You should have a positive idea of what you want."

Jenkins' style is often to tempt the batter with a pitch that looks better than it is. He will throw a pitch that looks good as it approaches the plate but then surprises the hitter—it is faster or slower than it seemed to be, or it dips or curves outside of the batter's hitting zone.

"The important thing that I've learned is that the hitter will swing at a pitch if he sees it. If you continually throw the ball away, he's not going to swing. So you've got to make the pitch hittable so the hitter can pick it up and swing at it."

This is a dangerous strategy, though, because of the risk of serving up a pitch that is too easy to hit. "You don't want to make the pitch right there," Jenkins says, indicating a spot in front of his waist. "Not right down Broadway." His margin of error on the mound is slim.

As a control pitcher, Jenkins also tries to pitch away from a hitter's strengths. Very good hitters, he says, have no glaring weaknesses. But nearly every hitter, he says, has a pattern—of swinging at the first pitch, trying to pull the ball with two out, or guessing fastball when the pitcher falls behind in the count. He tries to uncover each batter's pattern. Some examples:

Steve Garvey: "Steve Garvey is totally a fastball, first ball hitter. You don't try to throw a fastball by him on the first or second pitch because he's always swinging. So you try to feed him some off-speed pitches inside, and get him off the plate, and then go away from him."

Darryl Strawberry: "He likes to swing at pitches out over

the plate and pitches away, but I think they're trying to jam him now. He's going to have to learn how to hit the inner half of the plate and become a pull hitter. The book is to get ahead, maybe with a breaking pitch, then go away with hard stuff, then jam him up."

Mike Schmidt: "Mike Schmidt is off the plate. He likes to extend his arms. He likes to drive into the ball. You have to basically pitch him down and give him off-speed pitches. But then he'll prove you wrong. You throw him curveballs down and away and he adjusts and reaches out there and drives a lot of balls hard to right and right-center field. So you have to be very careful."

Talking about Schmidt, Jenkins makes a different point about patterns. Just as he labors to find the hitter's patterns, he tries not to reveal any pattern of his own that would shift the advantage to the batter. He will even go so far as to play mind-games with the batter. Jenkins, for example, sometimes shakes off a sign, even though he intends to throw the pitch the catcher has asked for, as a way of getting the batter to wonder what is going on. He just loves to be ahead of a hitter by an 0–2 or 1–2 count.

"You've got to make him think a little," he says. "So you maybe throw him an off-speed pitch inside or a fastball inside just to make him think that now you're going to go away with your best pitch. Then you come back with the same pitch you brushed him back with—just to make him think a little more. So now the count's two-and-two, and now maybe he doesn't really know what your best pitch is going to be. You've made him think a little. He can't basically sit on one pitch the whole time."

He says that, even as a veteran, he spends as much time as

ever studying the game. "You should learn something every time you play," he says. "Every time you learn something, it helps you—maybe a week, month, maybe a year from now. Once you stop learning—let me tell you—you're going to be in the second row looking at somebody else playing."

Jenkins has, in a sense, moved into what could be called the third phase of his pitching career. He began as a thrower who, while eager to learn, could get by with his natural ability. He flourished during the years when he threw hard and was also a smart pitcher. And, most recently, he has survived and occasionally pitched very well with his combination of smarts, control, and competitiveness.

Yet the most recent phase of Jenkins' career has settled into a new, complex, and mildly disturbing pattern of its own. Since his string of 20-game seasons ended in 1972, Fergie has pitched for ten years but has pitched very well in just three of them—1974, 1978, and 1982.

Each of his best seasons came at a time when he needed a good performance to silence the critics and, in the later years, to prolong his career—his best performances came when he needed them most. "My history," he once said, "has been that I have had some of my best seasons after adversity."

It is the flip side of that statement that is worrisome. For some reason, when Jenkins has been able to afford a subpar year, his performance has slipped. It is hard to know why.

One theory is that Jenkins is at his best when he is unfamiliar to the hitters. Two of his finest years—1974 and 1982—came after he went to a new league, and it may be that he is smart enough to figure the hitters out before they can unlock his secrets.

It may also be that Jenkins relies, more than most pitchers, on his mental toughness—that is, his ability to concentrate at all times—to get batters out. Maintaining a consistently high level of concentration each year is very difficult. He has appeared in more than six hundred ballgames over eighteen years, and each one takes a mental as well as a physical toll on a pitcher.

Jenkins also has not been in a tight pennant race—with the accompanying pressure that helps bring out the best in many players—since the late 1960s. He does not possess the star quality that brings people out to the park to cheer him on. And, in recent years, he has become financially comfortable.

Such speculations may be unfair to a pitcher who has won so many games, struck out so many batters, and come back so many times. But they are not intended to undercut Jenkins' magnificent accomplishments. They are, rather, an attempt to show how hard his job has been—just how hard it is to be a consistent winner, especially on losing teams, year after year.

Whatever the explanation, following his fine season in 1982, Jenkins is on his way to another frustrating season in 1983. He starts off okay: in his first eight starts, he allows no more than three runs in five- or six-inning stints, but picks up just one win. One afternoon, he throws nine innings against the Phillies and gives up just one earned run, but he leaves the game before the Cubs win in extra innings.

He picks up his second victory June 4, beating Pittsburgh, 5–2, and supplies some of the punch himself with an RBI single in the second inning. In his next start, Jenkins shuts out the Cardinals, 7–0, on four hits. The complete game is the first by a Cub pitcher in 1983, and the team is on a hot streak, having won seven of eight games.

Jenkins continues to pitch fairly well in June, though he gets no closer to his 300-win goal. The games he starts tend to be close, but by the sixth or seventh inning he is usually removed for a pinch hitter. By the end of June, the Cubs have an 8–6 record in games that he has started, while Jenkins is 3–3. His earned run average of 4.20 is nothing to boast about, but no cause for alarm either.

However, things take a definite turn for the worse in July. The Cubs take a West Coast trip after the All-Star break, and Jenkins is awful. He is knocked out of two games in the early innings. There is talk of moving him to the bullpen.

"There is nothing wrong with me," he says. "I'm fine. If I wasn't, I wouldn't go out there." He says a mild hamstring pull, which he suffered earlier, isn't affecting his play. He pitches a little better in his next two outings but still can't manage a win.

Partly it is the fault of his teammates, who fail to score for him, but there are also signs that his concentration is off—he loses, 4–1, to the Mets by giving up two home runs to New York's rookie pitcher, Walt Terrell. A week later, he loses to the Mets and Terrell again, in a 2–0 heartbreaker.

By now, Jenkins is beginning to doubt himself and his teammates. He is no longer thinking about his pursuit of 300 wins; he just wants to hold onto his job.

"Three hundred is very important, but right now I'm not winning. That's the biggest thing you think about," he says. "You're not winning, and then you're not helping the ballclub, and then there are other youngsters in the organization who can possibly win.

"I went out this year, and I've got thirteen no decisions, and my record's 3–8, and it seems like I'm getting one run, two runs, no runs. We've had the opportunity to score runs a lot of times with the bases loaded one out, or bases loaded and nobody out, and we didn't score, so you kind of wonder when your team is going to score. There is a lot of pressure on you because you've got to keep holding that other team to as few runs as possible.

"I've played almost four months of baseball, and I've got three wins," he says. "I used to get three wins in three starts."

His coaches and managers speculate about what is wrong. They produce charts showing that he is relying too much on his curve and changeup, and not throwing enough fastballs. But his problems continue when he throws the fastball more.

"He pitched well early and didn't get any runs," Billy Connors, the team's pitching coach, says. "Then he got non-aggressive midway through the year. He got to a point where he didn't use his fastball enough and he paid for it. They sat on the breaking balls and took him the other way, and they hurt him."

Lee Elia, the manager, says, "In all fairness, Fergie has pitched very well on many occasions, but we just didn't get him any runs. That can be trying for a guy who's trying to win 300 ballgames."

On August 22, Elia is fired and replaced by Charlie Fox. It is, in effect, an admission by the Cub brass that the team has no chance of winning the pennant in 1983. The focus shifts toward building for 1984.

Jenkins has just pitched his second shutout of the year, defeating Atlanta, 3–0, and he beats Houston a couple of weeks later to improve his record to 5–9. He leaves that game early, however, when he becomes exhausted after running out a triple. "We've been after Fergie," Fox observes. "He's been getting a little heavy."

A week or so later, Jenkins is removed from the starting rotation and sent to the bullpen. The explanation: he's getting old.

"I think time is catching up a little bit with Fergie," Fox

says. "Instead of being a nine-inning pitcher, he's more a five-inning or six-inning pitcher now. I have some young people that I have to look at. He's a pro. He will accept that decision. He knows what it's for."

Jenkins, of course, has no choice but to accept the decision. Clearly he is not happy with it. "I'm in limbo," he says. "I'm not sure whether I'm going to start again or not." He is used sparingly during September, and he pitches ineffectively.

His year-end statistics are dismal—6 wins, 9 losses, just one complete game, a 4.22 earned run average. Only 1981, which was cut short by the strike, was worse.

The 1983 season, it turns out, has frustrated many of the older players who had been saluted in the spring when people were writing about baseball's Golden Age. Jim Kaat and Gaylord Perry, the oldest of the pitchers, retire before the season ends. Carl Yazstremski calls it quits; so does Johnny Bench, at thirty-five.

The Phillies, who had been dubbed the Wheeze Kids, win the National League pennant, but they do it by relying on younger players and resting old-timers Joe Morgan and Pete Rose. Rose is even removed from the starting lineup in one game of the World Series, and he is released by the Phils in the fall. So is Morgan.

Jenkins will turn forty in December, but he wants to play for at least one more season. He has 284 wins—putting him nineteenth on the all-time list—and he still hopes to reach 300. He has not given up, either, on his other dream—to play for a pennant-winning team. Despite the frustrations, he still enjoys playing.

"I love baseball," this big, unemotional but sad-eyed man says one afternoon. "I haven't told myself it's my life, but I fell in love with the game when I was seventeen years old. I married and I had three beautiful kids, but I'm also married to baseball. I'm married to this uniform.

"I'm nearly forty years old, and I've spent a little more than half my life playing this game," he continues. "I have to stop within a year or so, and I know I have to stop, but while I'm doing it, I know that this is what I want to do."

The farm beckons but so does the game. He talks in vague terms about coaching, possibly for the Detroit Tigers, who play close enough to his home that he could live with his family and still be part of baseball.

He thinks for a moment about a spring without the game and says he can't imagine what that would be like. "You have to miss it," he says. "You'll always be anxious to possibly go to spring training or to play."

How will he feel about being out of uniform, probably sometime soon, when a new baseball season begins? What will he do? That, Ferguson Jenkins says with a smile, is an easy question to answer. "I'll probably take Opening Day off and go to Detroit and watch a ballgame."

# The Perfectionist: *Bill White*

It was the summer of 1953, and Bill White, a raw young kid of nineteen, felt like he was on top of the world. He had been a star athlete and a fine high school student in Warren, Ohio, and he had just begun an equally promising career at Hiram College. He excelled in all sports and did well enough in class to make the dean's list. "I could have done, really, anything I wanted to do," he remembers.

White chose to pursue a career in baseball for a very practical reason: the money. The New York Giants wanted to sign him and offered a bonus of $2,500, enough to pay his college tuition of $700 a year and to repay his mother, who had gone to work to put him through school. "It wasn't much, but it was an awful lot of money to me," he says. "That was more money than I ever dreamed of back then."

No amount of money, though, could compensate White for the difficulties he would soon face. The Giants assigned him to a minor league team in Danville, Virginia, in the Carolina League, and he couldn't help noticing something on the day he reported to training camp: he was the only black on the team.

BRUT

Things soon got worse. As the season began, at a time when strict separation of the races was the law in the South, White found that he was the only black player in the entire Carolina League. Traveling through the low minor leagues is bad enough, but when you have to eat alone, stay in a different hotel from your teammates, and put up with all kinds of abuse every time you take the field—well, it's hard to imagine a rougher introduction to the game. White says, with some bitterness, "I was called names I had never heard."

Coming into baseball under such trying circumstances, White nevertheless managed to play well enough to rise quickly through the minor leagues. He went on to a successful major league career, and when it ended he had a number of choices open to him, including a chance to become a minor league manager. He left baseball briefly but soon returned to become a broadcaster with the New York Yankees. He has been doing play-by-play of Yankee games for thirteen years.

So, some thirty years after beginning his career in baseball, White's life still revolves around the game. Its rhythms and routines are his: he travels from city to city, spends most days in hotel rooms or at home, and heads out to the ballpark at night. His work year begins with spring training in the South, stretches through the hot summer months of July and August, and ends in the first cool days of fall, back home.

You might think, given his long association with baseball, that White has over the years developed a love for the game to which he is so closely tied. You might think so, but, at least according to White, you would be wrong.

The closest White comes to voicing affection for the game is when he makes the statement that "baseball is the best of all sports." That, however, is merely his opinion that baseball is more challenging and exciting than other sports. Beyond that, White insists that he has no deep feelings about the game: "I can't say, hey, I love baseball. I never really had an attachment to it."

White says, in fact, that he has stayed with baseball for all these years for exactly the same reason that he signed on in the first place: to make money. He has five children and enjoys living well, and he earns a good salary with the Yankees—far more than the $50,000 or so he earned most years as a player.

"I'm hooked only because perhaps at this point I'm making more money than I ever made before," he says. "You just don't take that and throw it away when you've got two or three more kids who are going to have to go through college."

White sees himself as a realist, not a romantic. He enjoys playing that role in the broadcast booth, especially when paired with longtime Yankee Phil Rizzuto, who is an unabashed booster for the team. During a game, Rizzuto will croon about some wonderful play by a Yankee, and White, cool and unemotional, will observe that it really wasn't all that spectacular.

Yet White, realistic and unsentimental as he may seem, is a perplexing man. He feels strongly, for example, that baseball—the game, remember, to which he says he has no attachment—isn't played today the way it ought to be played. He finds it difficult to remain a detached observer of the game. "It's not easy to watch games," he says, "especially when you've played the game—and when you've played at a certain level, and you see things happening below that level."

He says multi-year contracts have taken the pressure off ballplayers. He says today's players don't work hard enough or play hard enough or understand the game as well as the players of his time. And, provided that the cameras aren't pointing at him, he will shake his head in disgust when a player fails to execute a rundown play or cannot bunt the ball.

White is a perfectionist. "There are ways everything should be done," he says. He worked to develop his own skills, first as a player and then as a broadcaster, and he expects others to do the same.

So take him at his word—accept the fact that this man does his job because he makes a good living, that he wouldn't miss it if he had to stop tomorrow.

Bill White may not love baseball. But, love it or not, he cares very deeply about the way the game is played.

As a young boy, Bill White never dreamed of becoming a big league baseball player. It would have been a foolish dream. No black played in the majors until Jackie Robinson broke the color bar in 1947, and by then White had already turned thirteen.

Born in Florida, White was raised in the steel town of Warren, Ohio. His family had come north to join relatives who had settled in Ohio, and his father went to work in the steel mills. White says the family had enough money to get by but no more.

"We weren't poor," he says. "I always had enough food. I always had enough clothes. I didn't have extra money. But, back then, the families all pitched in and helped."

White, an only child, always liked sports, though as a kid he was too small to star. Still, in the neighborhood where his family settled, sports—and especially football—were seen as a way to escape life in the steel mills.

"We were basically football-oriented, because you could get out of the ghetto by playing football. I played football because that was a way to get a football scholarship," White says. "Base-ball still doesn't give the kinds of scholarships you can get in basketball or football."

White grew much bigger in high school—he is now 6 feet 1 inch and just a few pounds over his playing weight of 185 pounds—and he won the quarterback job on the football team. Encouraged by his parents to study hard, White averaged 3.93 out of a possible 4.0 and finished second in his senior class of 127. He was offered full college scholarships by a number of schools, including Columbia University in New York, but chose to go to Hiram, a small, well-regarded liberal arts college near home.

Baseball, meanwhile, had begun to interest him, though he didn't start playing until he was a teenager. First in high school and then at Hiram, White worked hard and began to shine as a player. He began as a pitcher but switched to first base after injuring his arm. Despite his great natural ability—strength, speed, hand and eye coordination—it took him a while to learn the game.

His break came during a 1952 state tournament sponsored by the National Amateur Baseball Federation in Cincinnati, where he was spotted by a part-time scout for the Giants. The Giants continued to scout him during the tournament finals in Cleve-land, and then immediately took him to Pittsburgh, where the Giants were playing the Pirates. He worked out with the team and was offered a contract on the spot. "The Giants along with the Dodgers had a history of being the first to bring in black people, so it was easy to sign with them," he remembers. "Monte Irvin was there. Willie Mays was there. Hank Thompson was there. Ruben Gomez was there. And Leo Durocher made me feel right at home."

When he reported to the Giants' training camp in Phoenix the next spring, White had his first problems with racial prejudice. He tried to go to a movie and was told that no blacks were allowed. (He still remembers the movie—it was *Cochise* with Stewart Granger.) Back at the hotel, he commiserated with Monte Irvin.

Playing for Danville, his first minor league team, there was no one to share the problems that confronted him virtually every time he looked for somewhere to eat or sleep. Worse was the abuse he had to take during the games. "I wasn't prepared for that," he says. "To have laws that I couldn't eat here or I couldn't drink there or I couldn't go to this bathroom. On the field it was even tougher, because you were just free game for whatever anybody in the seats wanted to say. There are some very ignorant rednecks in this country."

His teammates rallied behind him. "Teammates were good and the opposing players were good. There were some southerners I played with who helped me, and some southerners I played against who helped me as much as they could. But, basically, it was the people in the stands who probably wanted to show their neighbor they could holler at this nigger."

The Giant organization was not terribly sympathetic. At one point, when the racial climate was getting to him, White wanted to play somewhere else. "I said, hey, I don't have to play here. Send me someplace where I can live like any other citizen of this country." The team refused.

"The Giants, or any other club, were just not interested. They didn't care," White says. "They were sensitive only at the top, because you can make money for them at the top."

Somehow White turned the racism that he encountered to his advantage. "It just makes you want to do better. It motivated me. I wanted to show these people who felt they were mentally and physically superior to me that it was certainly not the case," he says.

"You can use it that way, or you can say the hell with it, or you can physically fight them. I'd rather say, hey, I'm going to become the best athlete and the best human being and the best scholar that I possibly can."

He hit .298 with 20 homers and 84 RBIs for Danville in 1953, good enough to move him up a notch in 1954 to Sioux City, Iowa, in the Class A Western League. The racial atmosphere improved a great deal, but there still were problems. White couldn't stay with the team in Lincoln, Nebraska, or Wichita, Kansas, and the memory of trying to find a place to eat one night in Wichita is still vivid.

"The whole team went in to eat, and you have to remember that in the lower minor leagues you're still eating in restaurants that are just a little bit better than truck stops," he recalls. "There were guys in here with grease all over them, no shirts on, or whatever. But they couldn't serve me. Or, they couldn't serve me with my group."

Manager Dave Garcia, who was kind that summer to White, led the entire team out of the diner. "We all said, fine; we got up and left," White says. "So we stopped in a little nicer place, and Dave went in and asked them if they could serve us, as a team, and the answer was no, again. But they had to eat, and I said, go on and eat. They did and they brought me something back out, which I don't think I ate." White says that was one of the few times in his life that he cried.

Garcia's memory of the incident is as clear as White's. He also remembers when, in spring training, White hoped that Marshall Bridges, another black player, would be assigned to Sioux Falls.

Bridges wasn't, making White the only black player on the team. On the first night of the season, Garcia shared a hotel room with White because he didn't know whether the white players would. Soon afterward, though, White made friends, and Garcia says now, "If you called every ballplayer on the 1954 Sioux City ballclub and asked them who the best-liked player on the club was, I think it'd be unanimous for Bill White."

What Garcia remembers most of all are White's skills as a player. "Best ballplayer who ever played for me, at any level of the game," the veteran baseball man says. "He was twenty-one years old and he led the league in home runs, led the league in stolen bases, hit over .300. There wasn't a doubt in my mind that he could be a successful major league ballplayer."

White made steady progress through the minor leagues. After hitting .319 with 30 homers and 92 RBIs in Sioux City, White moved up to AA ball with Dallas of the Texas League and hit .295, 22 homers, and 93 RBIs. He was already showing the consistency that would mark his big league career.

In 1956, White began the summer at the Giants' top farm club in Minneapolis, but played just twenty games before the call came from New York. He remembers his first game in the big leagues, and why shouldn't he? He hit a home run his first time up off a St. Louis Cardinal right-hander named Ben Flowers.

"Actually, he had me struck out," White says with a laugh. "On a 2–2 pitch, he threw a ball that I thought was on the outside corner. I started walking toward the dugout, and the umpire says, ball three. So the next pitch I hit up on the roof.

"The next time up," he says, "I missed another home run by about six inches. It was a double. But you've gotta remember that it was a real short fence in the old Busch Stadium in St. Louis. It was only about 326 feet to right-center field." He laughs again. "It was all downhill after that."

Actually, White had a decent rookie year. Playing mostly first base, he hit .256 with 22 homers and 59 RBIs as a strict left-handed pull-hitter. "That's why I didn't hit for a higher average," he says. "But, finally, after I went into the army and came back, I learned to hit the ball to all fields, and that's when my average started up."

His army service wiped out the 1957 season and nearly all of 1958 as well, though he did play twenty-six games for the Giants in their new home in San Francisco. During spring training in 1959, White was traded to St. Louis for pitcher Toothpick Sam Jones. White's arrival at the Cards' spring base in St. Petersburg, Florida, was not a happy one.

"I got off the plane and got a cab to their hotel and was told that I couldn't stay there," he says. "I had just left Phoenix, where everybody stayed at the Adams Hotel, one of the nicer hotels in Phoenix. To get to St. Petersburg and run into that right away wasn't pleasant."

The black players on the Cardinals and the Yankees, who also trained in St. Petersburg, were put up in the homes of black families while their white teammates enjoyed a good hotel. When the team broke camp and went north to St. Louis, things were only marginally better.

"St. Louis itself didn't have a good reputation," White says. "Even when I was there, St. Louis, racially, was quite conservative. I don't know how it is now, because I don't go back there. It wasn't the ideal place for a black guy to break in."

On the field, though, White was beginning to hit his stride. He started off slowly in 1959, and there was some grumbling from the fans as ex-Card Sam Jones starred for the Giants. White was still trying too hard to pull the ball and hit home runs.

With the help of batting coach Harry (The Hat) Walker, White shortened his stroke and began hitting to all fields. His average climbed so fast that he was named to the National League All-Star team as a left fielder. He finished the season with a .302 batting average, 12 homers, and 61 RBIs.

Once he returned to his natural position of first base, his fielding attracted nearly as much attention as his hitting. For a man weighing close to 200 pounds, White's quickness was amazing—he could scoop up grounders to his right, spear hard line drives, and block throws that were wild or in the dirt. In 1961, White matched a major league record by executing eight unassisted double plays—no mean feat for a first baseman.

White's hitting also improved steadily, a sign that the young player was constantly looking for an extra edge and working on his technique. His home run total climbed from 12 to 16 to 20, and his RBI total grew from 72 to 79 to 90 during his first three seasons with the Cardinals.

But White's peak years were still ahead. From 1962 through 1965 he was a consistent threat at the plate, and his statistics proved it. Batting averages: .324, .304, .303, .289. Home runs: 20, 27, 21, 24. Runs batted in: 102, 109, 102, 73. He had a closed stance and a quick stroke, and he could get around the bases in a hurry.

White was a confident hitter. "When I went into a season, first of all, I knew I was going to hit anywhere from .280 to .310 or .320. If enough people got on, I was going to drive in a hundred runs. I was going to score runs. I was going to win Gold Gloves. Those things I knew before the season started," he says.

For all his confidence, White never stopped working on his game—even during the off-season. Long before the Nautilus machine and the videotape camera became fixtures in big league camps, White was using similar tools to perfect his skills.

"I used to swing the bat two hundred or three hundred times a day," he says. "I'd look at movies of myself hitting. I'd work out, sometimes ten or twelve hours a day, playing racquetball to maintain quickness and keep my weight down. When I played, I stayed in shape twenty-four hours a day, twelve months a year."

His most satisfying season was probably 1964. White started slowly, as he had been prone to do, and he was hitting just .263 with 30 RBIs at the All-Star break. The Cards, too, had been slow out of the starting blocks. In mid-July they were buried in eighth place.

White and his teammates picked up steam all at once. He lifted his average and began knocking in runs, as teammates Ken Boyer and Dick Groat began hitting and Bob Gibson worked his way out of a slump. The Cards began playing like they had late in 1963, when they had won 19 of 20 in a late-season stretch to close within a game of the Los Angeles Dodgers, only to falter and finish in second place.

St. Louis fans were hungry. The team had endured eighteen seasons without a National League pennant, longer than any team except the Chicago Cubs. But with just twelve games to go in the season and the Phillies ahead by 6½, even the most loyal fans were ready to give up.

What followed was one of the maddest scrambles in baseball history. The Phils collapsed and the Cards got hot. Going into the last weekend of the season, St. Louis led Cincinnati by one game and Philadelphia by a game and a half.

St. Louis was hosting the last-place New York Mets, who had lost eight in a row. On Friday night, Al Jackson of the Mets outdueled Gibson to beat St. Louis, 1–0. Their lead shrunk to half a game.

The next afternoon, the Cards were awful. They made five errors, losing to the Mets, 15–5, and the pennant was up for grabs among all three teams on Sunday.

The Mets jumped in front of the Cards for the third day in a row, leading 3–2 in the fifth inning. But Gibson, entering the game in relief after just one day's rest, throttled the Mets as his teammates applied offensive pressure. White singled and scored in the fifth, and he smashed a two-run homer in the sixth to put the Cards in front to stay. They won, 11–5, and as their celebration began, some 3,000 fans gathered outside the clubhouse and refused to go home until Boyer, Lou Brock, Curt Flood, and finally White came out to take their bows.

The Cards were a special team, White remembers, a team without a dominant star and one where everyone contributed. "We had a lot of indians and no chiefs," he says. "Boyer and Musial, they were supposedly the leaders. Gibson was the needler. Flood was there. All the different personalities came together on the field, and they knew their jobs and there was no jealousy at all, for some reason. Possibly because we didn't know what the other guy was making. But everybody knew what their job was."

This, to White, represents the way baseball should be played. He described his own role. "My job was to drive in runs and play a decent first base. I batted third, so I didn't mind sacrificing a bit when it called for that, because Boyer was behind me and whoever was behind him could hit, too. It was a team, probably, without an ego. Even our manager, Johnny Keane, was a selfless person. You couldn't see him on the bench. He very seldom used the word 'I'."

White had played a crucial role in the stretch drive. He had knocked in 69 runs after the All-Star break and lifted his average 40 points to .303. He played in all but two games for the Cards, and won another Gold Glove.

The World Series that followed was a seven-game thriller, pitting St. Louis' pitching and defense against the power of the New York Yankees. The Cards won game seven behind Gibson, 7–5, salvaging an otherwise disappointing series for White. He had begun the Series in an awful slump—failing to hit in the first five games. He says now that it didn't bother him. "I went 0 for 19 doing the best I could," he says. "Nothing affects me. I did the same thing once during the season, and John [Keane] said, 'You're going to come out of it.' Luckily, I came out of it after four or five games of the Series."

White claims he took his slump in stride. "It didn't affect me at all. That's the way the better athlete is able to handle adversity. You just do the best you can. If I hit the ball hard and somebody catches it, my job is still to hit the ball hard. I'm not going to go and jump up and down and yell and scream because I hit the ball hard and the guy caught it. Because I'm going to hit one off the fists, and it's going to fall in." White broke out of his slump with 3 hits and 2 RBIs in games six and seven.

Years later, White was still remembered in St. Louis for something he did on the night the Series ended. Back when no one expected the team to reach the Series, he had agreed to speak at a church fundraiser in a nearby suburb. When the Series began, the church figured that White wouldn't make it and booked a substitute, a basketball coach from a local college. But White left the team party after game seven and arrived at the church, delighting the crowd and upstaging the basketball coach. "I felt sorry for him," White says, "because he had accepted the substitute role, and all of a sudden we had just won the thing and all St. Louis was sky high and they don't want to hear anything from him. It was an enjoyable night."

White's baseball career peaked in 1964, though he would play for five more years. His batting average and run production dropped off the next season, and the Cards slid to sixth place. In October 1965, White went to the Phillies in a blockbuster trade: White, Groat, and catcher Bob Uecker for pitcher Art Mahaffey, outfielder Alex Johnson, and catcher Pat Corrales.

White did well in his first summer with Philadelphia, hitting 22 homers and driving in 103 runs in 1966, but he tailed off in 1967 and was ready to quit. He says he was talked out of it by John Flynn, the Phils' general manager. "I don't know why," he says now, "because I couldn't play." He played part-time in 1968.

St. Louis re-acquired White in 1969. "I called the Cardinals and they said, come on out and pinch hit, we should win another pennant. What they really wanted me to do was to manage in the farm system," he says.

He had another frustrating season in 1969, coming to bat just 57 times and driving in 4 runs. "I couldn't play anymore and I wasn't enjoying the sitting," he says. This time, there was no question: he quit.

He was not sentimental about leaving the game. "When I got out of it, people would say, 'Everything you have you owe to baseball.' I said, 'Bullshit. I don't owe anything to baseball. Nor does baseball owe me anything. We're even. I played. I got paid. I'm not going around and saying what a great thing baseball is."

The Cards offered White the manager's job at Tulsa, the top team in their farm system. He also had work, if he wanted it, doing sports news on television newscasts in Philadelphia—an outgrowth of a part-time career in broadcasting that he had begun in the early 1960s.

By his own account, White became a broadcaster by accident. Joking around one day, he told Harry Caray, the play-by-play man for the Cardinals, what an easy job he had. Caray replied that he should try it. "He asked me to cut a demo tape, which I did, and he took it to Bob Hyland, and Hyland liked it, and that's how I started in radio."

Hyland, the general manager of KMOX–AM in St. Louis, was building a reputation for training ballplayers as broadcasters. Hyland had broken in Joe Garagiola, Bob Uecker, and Gibson, and remembers being impressed with White. "He had his head screwed on right, and he had his feet on the ground," says Hyland, who is now a regional vice president for CBS. "He was one fellow who looked at life seriously enough to think about what's going to happen after his glove had to be hung up."

Hyland felt that White was far more intelligent than the typical ballplayer. He says, "There was something—it was almost ethereal about him—so you got the idea that he was a thinking person. He wasn't going to do anything that would be stupid or embarrassing to himself on the air. You realized that, before he did a job, he would think it out."

White began as a jack-of-all-trades at KMOX. "I catalogued records. I did a disc jockey show where I was terrible. I did interviews, I filled in as host on talk shows. I got all kinds of experience," he says. "During the baseball season, I'd have a five minute interview show after the ballgames on Saturdays."

Hyland recalls that, even then, White's personality was unusual. Unlike other ballplayers who were beginning new careers as broadcasters, White seemed unattached to baseball. In general, he expressed few emotions and took a crisp, businesslike approach to his job.

"He was a very cold guy," Hyland says. "That was the unusual part of Bill. The other fellows that we've gone through had a warmth to them and it [baseball] made a difference to them. Bill's personality was such that he didn't allow that."

From the start, he dedicated himself to becoming a good broadcaster. "He has a pride that's very, very evident," Hyland says. "He did tape recordings and tape recordings and tape recordings until he got it right. He was testing himself all the time."

When White retired, he was ready to try broadcasting full-time. He saw the new career as a welcome change, and also as a way to maintain his standard of living. The Cards paid their minor league managers about $15,000 a year, with no guarantees of longer employment.

"First of all, it was a challenge," he says. "Everybody thinks that jocks can't put words together. It was a challenge to become the best broadcaster, period, not just the best jock broadcaster. Secondly, it's a nice way to make a living. I make more now than I made when I played."

White became a sportscaster at WFIL–TV, an ABC affiliate in Philadelphia, appearing on the evening news. He wasn't very happy, however, with his limited air-time. "I got tired of working three minutes a day and putting in twelve hours to do that," he said.

Late in 1970, White let it be known that he wanted to try something else. He was approached by Mike Burke, then the president of the Yankees. "I told him, 'Hell, I've never done baseball.' They wanted a tape of my work in Philadelphia, I suppose, to see what kind of voice I had. The next thing I know, in January of 1971, we struck a deal, a one-year deal. I've been here ever since."

It was ironic that White found himself with the Yankees. The Yankees and the Cardinals had engaged in a spirited spring training rivalry when both trained in St. Petersburg in the 1950s and early 1960s. White remembers the New Yorkers as a privileged bunch who didn't play the hard-nosed, hustling brand of baseball associated with the National League.

"To be honest, I always disliked the Yankees," White says. "We played them all the time, and we felt they didn't work hard enough. They knew they were going to win so they'd go to spring training and loaf through it. We had to work our ass off. So we just beat their butts in spring training if we could."

Nevertheless, in his first season in New York, White sometimes found himself in a Yankee uniform. In an effort to get to know the players, he would throw batting practice and work out with them before the games.

In the broadcast booth, White joined Frank Messer, a veteran broadcaster, and Phil Rizzuto, the former shortstop who has been with the team as a player or broadcaster since 1941. Both were well-established in New York, and White was a somewhat uneasy newcomer. "When I first started out, I was nervous," White says. "You can't do anything being nervous. You don't know what is good broadcasting and what is not good broadcasting."

He remembers, for example, sitting in his chair and, because of his size, finding it hard to bend over comfortably and talk into the microphone. But he didn't want to complain.

"When you're nervous and you're working like that, your

voice is higher, tinny." But, typically stubborn and determined, he told himself, "If Frank and Phil can work with that mike, then, hell, I can work with that mike."

White eventually asked for, and got, a new microphone that made life easier. Twice a week, meanwhile, he took voice lessons and was coached in such techniques as staring into the camera's eye so viewers at home think you're talking to them.

Messer was impressed with White's diligence. "Bill would tape-record his segment of every game on radio, and on his way back—he had a two-hour commute to his home—he would listen to it on his car stereo," Messer says. "That was something that, to be honest with you, I never did even when I first started."

Harder than the technical aspects of broadcasting was the creative side—learning how to describe the game in a lively, accurate manner. "My first year, I was terrible. I had no style," White says. "The second year, I was a little bit less terrible. Each year you try to improve."

White learned, for example, not to get fancy when describing a game. "You can't use words that people don't understand. I will not use a word that 90 percent of the people can't understand," he says. "The simpler you are, the better you are. I would not like to hear Bill Buckley do a baseball broadcast."

He also learned that it is not the broadcaster's job to inject excitement into a game. "When we all start, we're up all the time. Everything—a routine ground ball, whatever—is a great play, or at least in your voice it is. But you learn that a routine ground ball is a routine ground ball, and a great play is a great play. You learn how to use your voice."

After some years, White became comfortable behind the microphone and won a reputation as a smooth and knowledgeable broadcaster. He was given a couple of part-time trials at the network level, first as a sportscaster on the "Today" show at NBC and then for a couple of seasons doing baseball games for ABC. Though he fit those assignments around his play-by-play work for New York, it appeared as if he might leave the Yankees for a more prestigious and demanding job at a network. Neither ABC nor NBC, however, offered a full-time job. He quotes one network executive as telling him, "Half of your shows are good, half of them bad. If you were in baseball, .500 would be pretty good, but unfortunately you're in TV, and that isn't any good."

So after thirteen years as a team, White, Messer, and Rizzuto have become fixtures in New York. Their personalities are familiar to Yankee fans, partly because baseball is a slow game, played every day, that invites the announcers to pass the time with conversations and anecdotes.

Messer says, "Football is different. You run a play, you analyze a play, you have a rerun. In basketball, the ball is in play all the time. In baseball, you really have more time to editorialize or entertain." The game has a tradition of storytelling.

The interplay among the broadcasters enlivens many games. Messer is well-prepared, straightforward, and professional. Rizzuto is excitable and unpredictable, a raconteur whose tales sometimes drift far from the game. White is a cool and thoughtful observer, dissecting the game from a distance.

"Bill tends to be more analytical, perhaps more critical of a player," says Messer. John Gordon, a Yankee radio broadcaster, says, "His strong suit in the broadcast booth is the ability to analyze and criticize and bring out the strategy of the game for the listener." He thinks White would have made an excellent manager.

When asked to describe his style, White says, "I'm not a fan.

I try to be the eyes of the people listening. I hope they believe me, and I think they do.

"When I say it's a long drive, it's not a popup. If a Yankee makes a horseshit play, it's a horseshit play. There's no excuse for it. I'm not going to say, well, the ball hit a pebble. I think what I do is simply a straight ballgame, and try to tell the fan a little more because of some of the situations I've been in."

White often refers to his playing days as he broadcasts a game, and his strong opinions grow out of his experience as a player. He believes, for example, that the players today are nowhere near as aggressive as his contemporaries. When he played first base for the Giants, they had Orlanda Cepeda and Willie McCovey in the minor leagues, trying to take his job away. "Now there are very few good players in the minor leagues. And who's going to push when a guy has a five-year contract?" he says.

White is equally blunt when it comes to another favorite theme: the need to restore the brushback pitch to its proper place in the game. One summer night, White faulted the umpires for warning the Yankees and Tigers that their pitchers could be ejected from the game if they threw too far inside. "You know what they're going to need on each ballclub soon?" he told Rizzuto. "A lawyer.

"This is really getting to be a tough game," he went on. "You've taken one third of the plate away from both pitchers now. A pitcher can't afford to throw the ball inside because he could make a mistake and be ejected from the ballgame." He added that the Detroit pitcher, Jack Morris, couldn't throw inside pitches to New York's Dave Winfield, who likes the ball on the outside of the plate so he can extend his long arms. Sure enough, a moment later, Winfield hit a two-run homer on an outside pitch.

White sounds almost nostalgic when he talks about the brushback wars during his playing days. He and Bob Gibson were roommates and close friends on the Cardinals, but both like to tell the story about the first time they faced each other after White was traded to Philadelphia. White leaned over the plate to go after an outside pitch, and on the next delivery Gibson hit him in the elbow. Unsmiling.

"Now, I knew that guys were going to throw at me. They did. They'd try to hurt you," White says. "But you got out of the way. I got hit in the head once. I got hit in the back a couple or three times. But that's life. One letter-writer said to me, 'You try to be macho.' And maybe that's what it is. But that's the way it used to be."

Despite his inclination to speak out, White has to watch what he says on the air. His goal of doing a "straight ballgame" is not as easy as he makes it sound.

For one thing, local broadcasters, unlike announcers for the networks, serve at the pleasure of the teams they cover. White, Rizzuto, and Messer are paid by WPIX, the station that televises the Yankees, but they are hired and can be fired by the team. White acknowledges this, but says the Yankees and their owner, George M. Steinbrenner III, have never interfered with him. "To be quite honest with you, and I tell a lot of people this, Steinbrenner, outside of one time, has never tried to tell me what to say."

He claims that the one attempt by Steinbrenner to influence the broadcast—the issue was a Yankee pitcher named Dock Ellis—actually backfired. "He didn't particularly like Ellis, and I was saying a few too many positive things about Ellis for him," White says. "So I just said more positive things. Since he didn't like it, I just went the opposite way. Since then, we haven't had any problems."

Still, White is careful, especially when it comes to the weaknesses and mistakes of individual players. Between innings, White and Rizzuto will pick apart a game—critiquing the style of play, the managers, and the errors. He says, smiling, that the conversations that unfold in the booth when the microphones are turned off would make "an interesting broadcast."

One time, the Yankees had a runner trapped between first and second base, and catcher Thurman Munson threw the ball to second, allowing the runner to return safely to first. "I'm trying to figure out why," White says. "You've got to run at the guy and stop him, make him commit himself one way or the other. Then I looked at Munson's record. And he'd only played one year in the minor leagues. He'd never even *seen* that play before. Now I can excuse that. But baseball can't. Because it didn't allow him to learn his craft."

But White rarely criticizes an individual player on the air. For all his disapproval of the modern-day player, White continues to identify with the men on the field.

"I know how hard it is, because some goddamn balls have gone through my legs to lose a ballgame. That's happened to me—not often—but it's happened," he says. "I'll say, hey, it was a bad play, the guy didn't get his glove down, or whatever, but I'm not going to say, hey, that guy's making $500,000, he's gotta catch that. What I have said, when I see official scorers give base hits on balls that should be played, is, wait a minute, a major leaguer is expected to make that play. I say that but I leave it there."

White, in essence, has developed a code language to communicate his feelings about a game. He won't, for instance, fault a player for failing to "hustle," but he will say, "He should have left home plate running on that popup." He won't second guess a manager, but he will try to illuminate the strategy of a game. "I will say, maybe, there's a left-handed batter up after this one and the bullpen is empty. Now what I'm saying is, why in the hell doesn't he have a left-hander warming up in the ninth inning. I will allow the fan, if he knows baseball, to understand what I'm saying."

To achieve this kind of subtle communication, White must exercise considerable restraint and control in the booth. He has had a lifetime of practice at those skills. From his minor league days as a black player in the South, when hecklers in the stands goaded him, White learned to hide his emotions. To become upset or to fight back would have been a sign of weakness. As a big league player, he worked every day, year-round, at every aspect of the game. He patiently endured the inevitable slumps, even when they came in the glare of the World Series. And, finally, as a broadcaster, White started all over again, a rookie at thirty-five. He holds himself to high standards, trying to provide a credible account of the game without breaking the hazy, unwritten rules of local broadcasting.

Through it all, White says he has been motivated by money, and, in fact, he has provided well for his family. But, clearly, there is more to it than that. Burning inside this big, tough, soft-spoken individualist is a fierce desire to succeed—as a player, as a broadcaster, as a man.

"If you're going to do anything, you do it the best you can, no matter what it is," White says. "If you want to put that into the category of pride, that's fine. Whatever you do, you try to do it the best you can."

# Going Home: *Catfish Hunter*

Catfish Hunter is having a rough day. He gets up early in the morning, as usual, and drives over to a creek near his home outside Hertford, North Carolina, hoping to do some fishing. When he arrives, he finds that the water is still frozen from a long cold spell that has just ended. It is early January.

His next idea is to hunt for Canada geese, which pass through the area at this time of year on their way south. He sets off for the woods with a friend, and they spot a few geese, but the birds never come down to the ground. So they can't shoot at any of them.

Now facing him is a chore he had hoped to avoid—mowing down some millet that has grown too high on his farm. He heads for the fields behind his home on his tractor, called a bush-hog. Before too long, the tractor breaks down; something is wrong with the gears. The machine doesn't have to be fixed immediately, since the farm doesn't require much attention at this time of year. "Right now," Hunter says in a measured Carolina drawl, "you don't have to farm. It's good to get things ready. But you can pretty much do what you want to."

Still, figuring that the day is pretty much spent, he climbs

into his pickup truck and heads over to the John Deere distributorship to buy new parts for the gear. He makes a right turn out of his driveway and begins a five-mile trip to Hertford that he could drive with his eyes closed. For one thing, the road is practically straight, and for another, he has traveled back and forth over it since he was a boy.

This northeastern section of North Carolina, known as the Albemarle, is farm country. Flat land, now barren but soon to be planted with corn or soybeans or peanuts, extends away from the road in both directions. The farmhouses and homes are modest wood structures, and a few look rickety. Between the farms are deep woods, crisscrossed with dirt paths used by hunters.

On the way to town, Hunter points out some familiar landmarks: the remains of the house where he grew up, which was destroyed by a fire several years ago; the home where his wife, Helen, grew up and where her mother still lives; the town hall, where his oldest brother, Marvin, is the town clerk; and the Little League field where he coaches one of the teams and where his son, Todd, learned baseball.

Downtown Hertford has a certain charm. Its Main Street is lined by about a dozen stores, including a five-and-ten that looks like it hasn't changed much since the 1930s. People stop to pass the time of day in front of the Perquimans County Courthouse or in Woodard's Drug Store. This is the kind of town where everyone knows everyone else, and a stranger attracts attention.

Hertford looks like any small town in America except for a small detail on a mural that some school children painted on a building on Main Street. There, near the pictures of farm life and hunting and the town's most famous landmark, an S-shaped bridge over the Perquimans River, is an emblem of the town's most famous resident: a blue-and-white New York Yankee cap.

James Augustus Hunter spent fifteen years playing major league baseball, first for the Kansas City and Oakland A's, and then for the New York Yankees. For a while, he was one of the best-known, most talented, and richest ballplayers in America. Hunter played for two famous teams—famous not only for their pennants and world championships but also for the arguments and controversies that marked their conduct off the field. They were famous as well for their owners, Charles O. Finley and George M. Steinbrenner III, who made the headlines as often as their players. These teams did not merely play ball; they created dramas.

Hunter, a mild-mannered and good-natured man, was more likely to be a peacemaker than a brawler on both teams. He figured in a big controversy only once, and it involved a contract dispute with Finley that made him baseball's first free agent, a rich man, and a Yankee. He was, for a while, by far the highest-paid player in baseball history, and even now he can afford to live wherever and however he wants. He has chosen to return to Hertford and to live simply. His friends and relatives say that, in some ways, he never left home.

Born April 18, 1946, Hunter was the youngest of nine children. His father, Abbot Hunter, was a tenant farmer who grew corn, peanuts, and soybeans, the staples of farms in Hertford. The family was neither rich nor poor; they just got by.

Everyone worked on the farm. "When we got our crop down, we'd go help other farmers," Hunter remembers. "We'd help people pull watermelons and cantaloupes. Working like that, you didn't think it was lifting weights, but you lift a 25 pound watermelon, 40 pound watermelon, throw it on the truck all the time, it's like messing with weights." Farm work was hard, but Hunter never stopped farming, even during his playing days. He would return each winter to Hertford to work with his brother, Pete, who took care of the farm while Jim was away.

Hunter looks like a farmer. Dressed this afternoon in a flannel shirt, faded green corduroys, and a beige windbreaker, he sits behind the wheel of his Ford pickup and waves or honks the horn when he sees a familiar face. His salt-and-pepper colored hair sticks out from beneath a John Deere cap that seems a bit too big for his head—a reminder of the way he used to push his baseball cap, which was also a little too big, back onto his head after each pitch. He chews Red Man tobacco and spits out his chaws into a plastic cup that he keeps under the front seat.

At the local Deere distributor, which is a few miles north of Hertford, Hunter gets a friendly welcome from a young man behind the counter. "You miss playing baseball, Mr. Hunter?" he says. Catfish replies, "A little bit." "Bet you don't miss Mr. Steinbrenner," the man says. Catfish chuckles. He gets back into the truck and gripes that the gear part for the tractor costs $64; rising prices bother even a millionaire farmer.

On the way home, Hunter points out the town's only industry, a shirt factory that employs about two hundred people. Hertford has not attracted any new businesses in recent years, and its population of 2,300 has remained steady. In fact, Hunter says, the town hasn't changed much since he was a boy, and that suits him fine.

As much as he loves baseball, Hunter's feelings about his home town made it easier for him to leave the excitement of Yankee Stadium behind and return to Hertford. His last season in the big leagues was his only unhappy one; he was removed from the starting rotation and won just two games. When the season was over, he decided it was time to quit. He was thirty-three.

He could have gone on, as so many older players do. They stay on to break one more record or win one more pennant or collect one more paycheck and spend one last summer with their buddies in the clubhouse.

Sometimes Hunter misses playing, and often he misses being around ballplayers. He doesn't, however, miss the limelight. "I don't miss the big cities either," he says. "I don't even like to go to Hertford. I'd rather stay home."

He is, essentially, a simple man, content with his life as a farmer. He likes to spend time with his friends and family. He is happy for the chance to watch his three children—Todd, fourteen, Kim, ten, and four-year-old Paul—grow up, and he enjoys hunting and fishing nearly as much as he enjoyed playing baseball.

For the past few days, Hunter has been thinking about just how much he enjoyed baseball. When Yogi Berra was named manager of the Yankees after the 1983 season, one of his first moves was to pick up the phone and call Hertford with an idea for an old friend. Catfish, he said, why don't you come back to New York and be my pitching coach? Catfish said he'd think it over.

The first man to ask Catfish Hunter to leave his farm was a fast-talking insurance man from Chicago named Charles Oscar Finley. In the summer of 1964, Finley drove his long, black limousine to the Hunter farm and began unloading Kansas City A's warm-up jackets and green baseballs, and handing them out to anyone who wanted one. In return, he wanted something, too: Jimmy Hunter's name on an A's contract.

Jimmy and his brothers had always loved baseball. "We'd ride to the Little League park and play, and then we'd play in the yard the rest of the time," he says. When it rained, they would go inside a barn, break up corncobs, and try to hit them with sticks.

Being the youngest of the nine children gave Jimmy an advantage; he was the most likely to be excused from farm chores to play ball. "I guess I had a better opportunity than they did because I didn't have to work as much as them. They did most of the work," he says, grinning.

But his brothers paid him back for that. When it came time to play, they wouldn't give him a chance with the bat. "I always had to throw strikes to my brothers for them to take batting practice. They wanted to hit, so I guess that's the reason I became a pitcher."

By the time he reached high school, Hunter knew how to pitch. He had good control, a rising fastball, and a sinking fastball. He didn't need much else.

In his last two years in high school, Hunter won 26 games and lost 2. He pitched a perfect game during his junior year, as well as four other no-hitters and one game where he struck out 29 batters in 12 innings. He also played American Legion ball, where the competition was much stiffer, and did just as well.

"I was a control pitcher even then," he says. "I knew where the ball was going all the time. We'd always watch the other team and see what they could hit: high ball, low ball hitters, whatever, just like the major leagues almost."

Since high school players could be signed by any major league team back then, the scouts began to find their way to Hertford. But Charlie Finley had a special weapon: a soft-spoken North Carolinian named Clyde Kluttz.

Kluttz, a former major league catcher who was then a scout for Kansas City, practically camped out at the Hunter home that spring. He softened the family up until the day Finley himself called on the telephone to finish the negotiations. Hunter, who was just an eighteen-year-old schoolboy, had no idea what to ask for, but he knew Finley had recently signed another young pitcher, Blue Moon Odom. He had also taken a shine to a fancy car that one of the scouts had driven. So Hunter told the owner: "I want the same contract Blue Moon Odom got. Plus I want a brand new Thunderbird car. Black." Finley said no to the car, but offered a $50,000 bonus, plus $25,000 if Hunter didn't make the major leagues and needed the extra money to go to college. He also demanded an answer right away. Hunter agreed to sign. "I'd never seen that much money before," he says.

Finley had one more question for Hunter. "Have you got a nickname?" he asked, as they put the finishing touches on the contract. When the boy said no, Finley found out that he liked to hunt and fish and told him, "Well, when you were six years old, you ran away from home and went fishing. About four o'clock, your mom and dad found you, and you caught two catfish and you were bringing in a third one. That's how you got your name. Now repeat it to me."

With that, Finley announced that he had signed the prized young pitching sensation, Catfish Hunter. Hunter figured getting a new name was part of being a professional ballplayer, and even now he doesn't mind being called Catfish. But, as he says with some amazement, "That man can sure change a man's life."

After a foot operation kept him from playing during the summer of 1964, Hunter pitched in a Florida instructional league the following winter. In 1965, as a player who had received a signing bonus of at least $40,000, Hunter was required by major league rules to be carried on the A's roster. He expected to spend the season on the bench before going to the minors to start his career in earnest, but the A's were such a weak team that Manager Haywood Sullivan decided he had nothing to lose by using Hunter.

Hunter pitched a couple of games in relief, and then blew a 7–0 lead in his first start. His first victory, which came on July 28 against the Red Sox, wasn't a pitching gem either. The A's won it, 10–8.

Before long, though, Hunter had won a place in the starting rotation and pitched some good games—especially considering that he was a nineteen-year-old with no pro experience. He finished with an 8–8 record for the last-place A's.

Hunter's performance pleased Finley and the A's brass. So did his attitude—he was an easy-going country boy who, after growing up in a big family in a friendly town, seemed comfortable with himself and secure about his future. Unlike some young pitchers, he didn't dwell on his defeats. He was certain that, sooner or later, he would become a winner.

"He has the right temperament for a pitcher," said Eddie Lopat, an ex-pitcher who was then an A's executive. "He's smart. He stays cool and tries to learn." The following spring —when Hunter had expected to be in the minor leagues learning the game—he was the Opening Day pitcher for Kansas City.

In 1966, Hunter was good enough to represent the A's on the American League All-Star team, though he didn't play. He made the All-Star team again in 1967 and probably wouldn't have played that year either if the game hadn't stretched into extra innings. With the contest tied at 1–1, Hunter was brought in to pitch in the eleventh inning. For four innings he shut down a batting order of National League stars. In the fifteenth, he gave up a game-winning home run to Tony Perez of the Cincinnati Reds to end the longest All-Star game in history.

Still, Hunter, then a crew-cut twenty-one-year-old, had made quite an impression in his first All-Star contest.*

Less than a year later, on May 8, 1968, Hunter took the mound for a night game against the Minnesota Twins at the Oakland Coliseum. Finley had moved the A's to Oakland in the beginning of 1968, Hunter's fourth season. Before the game, Hunter was in a fighting mood. "I was taking batting practice and the manager at the time was Bob Kennedy," he remembers. "He told me"—and here Hunter's voice becomes a snarl, imitating the manager—" 'Git out of the cage. You ain't no hitter. Let the hitters hit.'

"Well," Hunter says, "I could hit just as good as some of our hitters. Even Dick Green, our second baseman, said, 'Let him hit in front of me. Heck, I can't hit.' " (In the days before the designated hitter rule, Catfish was proud of his hitting. He batted .350 one season.) "I got out of the cage and I flung the bat a little ways and Kennedy says, 'Better watch it. I can goddamn fine you for that.' So I said, 'Go ahead.' I walked on into the clubhouse. I was mad."

He was mad enough to show the manager that he could hit. He doubled in the third inning, bunted safely to drive in the first run of the game in the seventh, and singled home two more runs in the eighth. On the mound he was even better; he was, in fact, perfect. Hunter retired every batter he faced, striking out 11 and allowing only five balls to get beyond the infield. It was only the tenth perfect game in major league history, and what made it all the more unexpected was that it was thrown by a little-known youngster, not by an established star.

---

* The game was the same one in which Ferguson Jenkins struck out six American Leaguers. See Chapter 7.

He still thinks the fight with Kennedy helped spur him on. "I wanted to show him that I could pitch and hit," Hunter says. "We beat 'em, 4–0, and I had three of the RBIs. Everything just went right."

Still, after several seasons in the major leagues, Hunter remained an inconsistent young pitcher who showed flashes of brilliance. His next outing after the perfect game proved that: he gave up a leadoff homer to Rod Carew and five more runs in the first inning.

By the end of 1969, after five seasons in the majors, Hunter had won 55 games and lost 64. He hadn't yet found his form.

He had trouble maintaining intensity on the mound. "I'd lose concentration and start to think about my record or something, maybe how I had this game in the bag and that gave me so many wins, and I'd make a careless pitch and they'd hit it and I'd wind up with a loss instead," he reflected at one point.*

Hunter insists that he was a better pitcher than his record shows in those early years. He says that, since he was not a strikeout pitcher, he needed a good team behind him. "The main thing at the time was that the Kansas City club didn't have any good players. We didn't have anything," Hunter says. His career began to jell at the same time the A's matured into an outstanding team.

Hunter, meanwhile, was becoming a pretty good match for Finley in their annual round of contract talks. Catfish never played baseball for the money, but his salary was a matter of pride, and he and the owner engaged in some stormy arguments.

"He loved to argue with you," Hunter recalls. "If he told you something and you said, 'Yes sir, yes sir,' he'd say, 'What

---

* Bill Libby, *Catfish* (New York: Coward, McCann and Geoghegan, 1976).

the hell is wrong with you? You know I'm telling you a lie.' He wanted you to argue with him."

Catfish obliged. After a season when he won 13 games and lost 17 for the last-place A's, he asked for a raise. Finley exploded, saying, "For what? You only won 13 games and you lost 17." When Hunter tried to argue that his earned run average of 2.80 was lower than the ERAs of several 20-game winners, Finley said that didn't make any difference. The next year, Catfish improved his won-lost mark but had a higher ERA. That fall, when he asked for more money, Finley shot back: "Look at your earned run average."

In 1970, Oakland made a strong run for the American League Western Division title but finished second to Minnesota. Reggie Jackson and Sal Bando hit home runs and drove in runs, Bert Campaneris sparkled at shortstop, Rollie Fingers became an effective relief pitcher, and newcomer Vida Blue threw a no-hitter. As for Hunter, he won more games than he lost for the first time, going 18–14 with a 3.81 ERA.

The next year, Hunter and Blue pitched the A's to the Western Division championship. Hunter went 21–11 with a 2.96 ERA while Blue was 24–8 with a sensational 1.82 ERA. But both failed in the divisional playoffs—Hunter allowed four home runs in a 5–1 defeat—and the Baltimore Orioles swept the A's in three games.

Oakland finally put it all together in 1972. Hunter led all the starters with a 21–7 record, six shutouts, and a 2.04 ERA, the lowest of his career, and this time Oakland saved something for the playoffs. By squeaking by Detroit in an exciting five-game series, the A's won their first pennant in forty-one years and advanced to the World Series.

By then, Oakland had developed its own style as a team. They were a young, energetic, individualistic crew, many of whom had sported mustaches and long hair since June, when Finley paid the players to grow them as a promotional stunt. Few, however, liked the owner, who would give players big bonuses to sign but then resist their demands for top salaries. They fought Finley and they fought each other, frequently and publicly. When Blue relieved Odom in the last playoff game against Detroit and then teased him about it, the two men came to blows during the victory celebration.

Hunter rarely got mixed up in scuffling, except to pry his teammates apart. His best weapon was his mouth—he enjoyed the banter around the locker room and was a master of the friendly put-down. Hunter also needled opponents; he was considered a good bench jockey.

Catfish was comfortable in the clubhouse. He would come out three or four hours before a night game, play cards for a while, or just talk. The routines, the companionship, even the rowdiness reminded him of the good times with friends back in Hertford. He once called the clubhouse "a home away from home."

Looking back, Hunter thinks the A's came together as a team in the locker room. While some clubs allowed rivalries and disagreements to smolder beneath the surface and then spill over into the game, Oakland's players did their fighting in the hotel or clubhouse and stuck together on the field. Hunter says Steinbrenner's Yankees operated much the same way.

"When you get twenty-five different people there and, with the coaches and everything, about thirty, and then with the owner, thirty-one"—he grins—"there's no way that everyone's going to think alike. So, when they had their differences, they just had a fight and that was it. Once we got on the field, it was a hundred percent baseball and that's all we thought about." The A's and Yankees emerged from their squabbling with a swashbuckling style and a deep sense of pride. They were brash and cocky and, like their owners, determined to win.

So the 1972 Series matchup of the A's and the Cincinnati Reds presented a pleasing contrast of styles: the feuding band of mustachioed, green-and-gold upstarts from California against the clean-cut, harmonious champions of the Midwest known as The Big Red Machine. Cincinnati was heavily favored to win.

After the A's won the opener, Hunter took the mound in the second game for the first time in a World Series. For eight innings, he shut out the powerful Reds on four hits. In the ninth, he allowed a run on two singles before Fingers came in to get the last out and save the 2–1 victory.

Aside from the perfect game, Hunter says that was the sweetest win of his career. When reminded that so many people expected the Reds to win, Hunter laughs and says, "We did, too. We thought they were going to win. But we just got out there and thought, whoa, we're in it now. We ain't got nothing to worry about. And we beat 'em two games in a row."

The Series turned out to be one of the most exciting of the 1970s, as all but one of the seven games were decided by one run. Hunter started the fifth game but wasn't involved in the decision, and he won the seventh game in relief. He called his two victories "the thrill of a lifetime."

In the early 1970s, Oakland established itself as the dominant team in baseball, and Hunter became one of the game's finest pitchers. In 1973, he rolled to a 15–3 record before injuring his thumb and sitting out three weeks. Still, he finished at 21–5, pitched two victories in the championship series against Baltimore, and one more in the World Series against the Mets.

He reached his peak in 1974, winning a league-high 25 games and losing 12. He crafted six shutouts. He won the ERA title with a 2.49 mark. And he was voted the Cy Young Award winner as the American League's top pitcher. In the World Series, Hunter won one game and saved one as the A's trounced the Dodgers for their third consecutive world championship. He was now 4–0 in Series play.

Despite his string of 20-game seasons and his post-season victories, Hunter's success still puzzled many fans. For one thing, he just didn't look impressive on the mound. He wasn't big or strong, and while his slider was better than average, he didn't throw hard and his curve ball was nothing special. Often, Hunter seemed lucky to win. Opposing batters would hit the ball hard or far only to see it caught. Many times they hit it so far that it couldn't be caught. Even in his best years, Hunter gave up lots of home runs—35 one season and 374 lifetime, more than any other pitcher in American League history. So batters were befuddled when they couldn't hit him. After Dave Bristol managed the Milwaukee Brewers to a frustrating loss to Hunter, he called a team meeting to tell his players that anyone should be able to hit a "puffball" pitcher like Catfish. One player yelled back, "Why in the hell don't you take a bat out there and see how good you can hit him?"

Hunter's secret was his superb control. On a good day, he could put the ball within an inch or two of his target. Such fine control was a potent weapon, especially when coupled with his willingness to study the hitters. "After you get your control, and you know what you're doing out there, you can make them hit your pitch and they're not going to get the good part of the bat on it," he says, making it sound simple.

Pinpoint control came naturally to Hunter. He spent hours

pitching as a boy and found a smooth motion that he never altered through his career. He would conceal the ball behind his glove, raise his left knee to his belt as he rocked back, take a medium stride, and throw three-quarters overhand.

"A lot of times they said they couldn't see the ball off me," he says. "The way I went through my motion, I always flipped my glove in front of the ball." By throwing every pitch the same way, he could get the ball where he wanted it.

Learning the hitters took more time. In his early years, he sat on the bench and charted pitches on the day before his turn on the mound—marking every pitch, its location, and result. "While you're doing that," he says, "You're finding out exactly what the guy is hitting.

"I knew the hitters—what they could hit and what they couldn't hit," he says. And strange as it sounds, nearly every major league hitter has at least one pitch that he does not like or cannot hit hard.

Take Reggie Jackson, who, fortunately for him, did not face Hunter often since they were teammates on the A's and Yanks. Batting against Hunter in a game in 1975, Jackson struck out twice and became so frustrated that he tried to bunt his last time up. Hunter explains, "If I knew what a guy couldn't hit—like Reggie, he can't hit a ball inside—that's the only thing I'd throw him, inside pitches. I'd throw it in there off-speed and they'd pull it foul. I'd throw another one in there with not as much on it, and they'd pull it foul. The next one I'd come in a little bit closer and throw it a little bit faster. They'd swing at it and miss it. If I got it in there, they couldn't hit it.

"I'd just try to move the ball around and change speeds all the time. That's the best way to pitch because they don't know where you're going," Hunter says. Watching him on a good day was a joy: together his pitches weaved an unpredictable pattern, each pitch deriving its effectiveness from the ones that came before. Jackson once said of Hunter, "He overpowers you with his control."

Hunter had trouble with only a few batters, and they tended to be high-average hitters who would try to drive the ball wherever it was pitched. Both Al Kaline and Rod Carew were tough outs for him. But by dominating the hitters whose weaknesses could be exploited, Hunter sometimes could get away with giving up hits to the stronger batters. He remembers pitching a playoff game for the Yankees against the Kansas City Royals in which he gave up three home runs to George Brett.

"I threw him three straight fastballs down the middle that day, and he hit three home runs. And Lou Piniella got all over me. He said, 'What the hell are you doing?' I said, 'Lou, how many runs did they score?' He said, 'Three.' I said, 'How many runs did we score?' He said, 'Four.' I said, 'That's all that counts, ain't it?' " To Catfish, that was all that counted.

Hunter expected to give up home runs. Since he had good control and rarely threw at hitters, they could dig in against him without worrying about being knocked down. Because it often took him a couple of innings to settle into a rhythm, he was especially vulnerable in the early innings—Pete Rose of the Reds, Wayne Garrett of the Mets, and later Davey Lopes of the Dodgers all led off World Series games against him with home runs. But the homers never bothered him.

"Most guys, they get mad or upset," he says. "But it's already over with. There's nothing you can do about it. You've got to start on the next guy." After giving up two homers in a Series game in 1974, Hunter joked afterward, "I had some friends here who'd never seen a homer, so I gave them a couple."

Hunter was unflappable on the mound—a carry-over from his remarkably calm off-the-field manner—and that helped him immeasurably. While baseball is occasionally an emotional game—think, for instance, of Jackson's ability to rise to the occasion in a World Series—pitching demands concentration and consistency more than emotion. A control pitcher like Hunter cannot afford to make too many mistakes, and he must take a steady, confident approach to his job.

"I can sum him up in one word. Cool," said Paul Lindblad, a friend and former teammate. "He never gets hot and bothered. He never gets excited. He's so calm, he calms you down. He's so confident, he gives you confidence."*

Hunter says, "I didn't ever get high and low. I just got out there and threw to spots and that was it." His success in post-season play did not result from any special intensity that he brought to those games. He says, "I always told them I was too dumb to get scared. I'd just go out there and pitch the way I always pitched. I just didn't think they could beat me."

Yet Hunter's control and his craftiness and his ability to stay cool did not make him famous; not even his perfect game or Series wins gained him the attention that was generated by a series of off-the-field events unprecedented in baseball history.

The events began with a mistake by Finley. The owner failed to make payments called for in Hunter's contract, and Catfish took the dispute to arbitration in late 1974. To the surprise of the baseball world, he won—and became the sport's first free agent. Baseball teams from across the nation soon dispatched emissaries to North Carolina to bid against each other in a wild auction for the pitcher's services.

---

* Bill Libby, *Catfish*.

It ended on New Year's Eve when, persuaded by his old buddy Clyde Kluttz, who was then a scout for the Yankees, Hunter decided to sign with New York. Hunter said, "To be a Yankee is a thought in everyone's head and mine. Just walking into Yankee Stadium, chills run through you."

Under the five-year contract, Hunter would be paid $100,000 a year in base salary. Another $50,000 a year would be invested for him. He would also get $100,000 a year for fifteen years after the contract expired, from 1980 to 1994. He got a $100,000 signing bonus. He even got a new car every year. Rather than going for big money at the time, Hunter decided to spread out the payments to provide for the long-term security of his family.

Hunter's contract foreshadowed a new era in baseball, when players were free to sell themselves to the highest bidder. But until free agency began in earnest in 1976, Hunter was in a class by himself as the sport's richest player. He showed, in his first season as a Yankee, that he was probably worth all the money.

For one thing, New York's attendance figures went way up. The Yankees attracted an average of 3,600 more fans on days he pitched than on days he didn't—enough, some said, to pay his first year's salary. Overall, the team drew more than 1.2 million at home, the most since they had won their last pennant in 1964.

On the mound, Hunter was as good as ever. His earned run average was only 2.58, and he pitched seven shutouts. His won-lost mark of 23–14 would have been even better with more support. (At one point, he lost two 1–0 games in a row.)

Even more notable was his durability. He led the league in complete games with 30 and in innings pitched with 328, and he needed just 20 innings of relief all season.

Hunter probably should have been rested more. He pitched on two days' rest one time in mid-September as new manager

Billy Martin tried desperately to rouse the slumping Yankees, who were 10 games behind. Hunter won the game, but the Yanks never got much closer and finished third. "They pitched me too much that first season, and it hurt my arm a little bit," he says now.

His problems didn't surface immediately. While Hunter slipped a little in 1976, winning 17 games and losing 15, his teammates picked up the slack. New York ran away from the rest of the division and won the first of a series of tension-filled playoff confrontations with Kansas City. Hunter won one game and lost one.

In the second game of the World Series in Cincinnati, Hunter turned in one of his most memorable performances. Unbeaten in Series play to that point, Hunter had nothing on the ball in the early innings and was roughed up for three runs. But after somehow escaping a bases-loaded, nobody-out jam in the third, he suddenly found his form. He became practically unhittable, weaving the ball in and out and up and down, changing speeds and spins, and thoroughly frustrating the Reds' hitters. The Yanks, meanwhile, tied the game, 3–3, and when Hunter retired the first two Reds in the bottom of the ninth, it looked as if the chilled crowd was in for a long night.

But Cincinnati's Ken Griffey slapped a slow bouncer up the middle where Fred Stanley, New York's shortstop, made a fatal mistake. Trying to get a little extra on his throw to nip the fleet Griffey, he flung the ball into the Cincinnati dugout. Joe Morgan was intentionally walked, Tony Perez drove the next pitch into left field for a single, and everyone went home, including a sorely disappointed Catfish Hunter. The loss was the only close game of the Series as the Reds swept the Yankees.

By the spring of 1977, Hunter's shoulder and upper arm

began to hurt nearly every time he pitched. It was hard for him to settle into his smooth, stylish motion, and his control was not nearly as sharp. Hampered by a foot injury and a urological disorder as well as his arm problems, Hunter staggered to a 9–9 won-lost mark and suffered some embarrassing moments. In a game against the Red Sox in June, he gave up four home runs before leaving in the first inning. He appeared in only one World Series game and was shelled for four home runs in a 6–1 loss to the Dodgers.

His next summer, too, was marked by arm troubles and some frightful outings. After missing six weeks of the season, he came into a game in Boston in the eighth inning and promptly gave up consecutive home runs to Fred Lynn and George Scott. "I hurt from the shoulder all the way down the arm," he said then. "I wish someone would cut it off." He went back on the disabled list.

Some days he could barely lift the arm. He says, "I threw so bad with my little boy one time that my wife told me, 'Let me throw to him. You can't throw.' And she can't throw a lick."

Desperate for help, Hunter agreed in mid-July to go under anesthesia and let the Yankee orthopedist, Dr. Maurice Cowen, manipulate his arm. It was a risky procedure, but it worked. "I went out that same afternoon, and I was throwing with my little boy and I said, 'It doesn't hurt,' " he says. When the pain returned a couple of weeks later, Dr. Cowen again stretched the arm to relieve it.

Amazingly, Hunter regained his form. In the second half of 1978, he reeled off eight wins, including a couple of shutouts and key victories down the stretch as the Yankees caught the Red Sox and then defeated them in a one-game playoff after the season ended. Hunter's teammates proclaimed, "The Cat Is

Back," and he finished with a respectable 12–6 record for little more than a half season's work.

In the Series against the Dodgers, Hunter lost the second game as he gave up a three-run homer to Ron Cey. But the Yankees, down two games to none, fought back as they had all year and swept three games in New York. Back in Dodger Stadium for game six, Catfish took the mound and won the finale, 7–2, with relief help in the late innings. "I felt great," he says. "I could have finished that game." With the rest of the Yankees, he had turned what looked like a lost season into a joyful one.

Hunter enjoyed New York—not the city, but playing with the Yankees. He lived in Norwood, New Jersey, a small town up the Hudson, and rarely ventured into Manhattan. One Hertford neighbor who visited said, "That was just like being in Hertford. If you didn't know any better, you wouldn't even know New York City existed." Catfish's oldest son, Todd, was six by then, and he traveled with his father on a couple of road trips each summer. The family spent the summers in New Jersey and the winters in Hertford.

But, much as he liked his stint with the Yankees, Hunter had always planned to retire when his five-year contract, signed in 1975, expired. "I told them I wanted to come home after that, and come back to the farm, and do what I wanted to do," he says. "That was long enough to play baseball—fifteen years." So he began the 1979 season expecting it to be his last. He wanted to leave at the top of his game.

It didn't work out that way. When Hunter dropped his first three decisions, he wasn't worried; he usually started slowly and improved as the season progressed. This time, he didn't get the chance. Veterans Tommy John and Luis Tiant, signed in the off-season by New York, displaced him in the rotation, and he never found his form. He recalls, "I'd pitch one week, then I'd wait three weeks. Finally, I went in there and I told Billy Martin that I can't pitch this way. He said, 'When do you want to pitch? I'll pitch you tomorrow.' I pitched the next day and then it was two or three weeks before I pitched again. There was no way that could work."

Hunter finished with a 2–9 record as the Yankees slid to fourth place. Had his season been more productive, he might have tried pitching for a year or two more. He was, after all, only thirty-three, and his arm felt fine again. Instead, gracefully and with his usual good humor, Catfish Hunter went home to Hertford.

It never really occurred to him to do anything else. "All my friends and neighbors are here. I like to hunt and fish, and everything I like to hunt and fish is here," he says. "There's no need to go anywhere else when everything you want to do is right here."

Leaving the center of Hertford, you can't miss the Hunter farm. The house is the biggest and newest around, and the barn has a big white baseball painted on it—only the seams and a horizontal line connecting them are left unpainted to form a rounded H. Inside are more reminders that the owner used to make his living playing ball. Pictures show him crew-cut and clean-shaven in a Kansas City uniform; shaking hands with President Ford in a locker room after a World Series game; arm in arm with his friend Reggie Jackson. Baseball bats that were used by teammates in the big leagues now form the balusters on his stairway.

Otherwise, though, this could be the home of any fairly

prosperous farmer in Hertford. A CB radio sits inside the front door, so that Hunter can stay in touch while he's out hunting or working the farm. Schoolbooks are piled on a table. Paul, his four-year-old son, has spread toys everywhere.

In fact, Hunter's life, for most of the year, is much like the life of any well-to-do farmer in Hertford. His children go to the same schools. His pastimes, hunting and fishing, are the same. And he grows the same crops—soybeans, peanuts, and corn—as his neighbors.

While Hunter is idolized by some people in Hertford, especially kids who grew up while he was pitching, older folks pride themselves on treating him just like anybody else. He is Jim or Jimmy or Mr. Hunter, and almost never Catfish. He is pleased that he has been able to pick up his life where he left it.

"He's a celebrity, but he doesn't act like a celebrity," says Charles Woodard, the local pharmacist, who has been friends with the Hunters since grade school. "I don't think he likes being recognized that much. He doesn't like all the pomp and circumstance that goes with it."

Hunter is a deacon in his church and a member of the Lions Club. The Lions raise money for the blind by selling baseballs, signed by Hunter, for $3 each in Woodard's Pharmacy. "He's really the same type of person that he was back in high school," Woodard says. "He's a good friend. He tries to help out lots of folks. He's a small-town boy, a country fellow like everybody down this way."

Hunter never liked big cities. He lived near Oakland for seven years and only went to San Francisco a couple of times to show visitors from Hertford around. He hated spending time in New York City. Still, Hunter enjoyed seeing other parts of the country. Without baseball, he says, "I might never have been out of North Carolina." Then he adds, laughing, "Well, I'd probably have been in Virginia a little ways."

He missed his hunting and fishing, his friends back home, and his family, but he loved playing baseball. "That was my life ambition, I reckon, to play baseball like that—traveling and meeting people and being around the ballplayers and everything. I loved it," he says. The best part was being with the players—"playing cards and sitting in the clubhouse in your underwear" is the way he puts it. While Hunter tends to be a private man with strangers, he loved the camaraderie that develops on a winning baseball team.

Even now, when asked about his playing days, he usually answers by telling a story—often a long and complicated yarn leading up to a humorous ending, marked by a hearty laugh. He has stories about all his old managers and teammates—Dick Williams, Alvin Dark, his friends Berra and Jackson and Piniella—and about the way he outfoxed this hitter or that one. Once he gets going, the memories really start to flow.

Berra's suggestion that he become the Yankee pitching coach brings back more memories. He is still fond of the Yankees—he roots for his old team, follows their games on television when he can, and usually makes a trip to New York each summer. Every year he enjoys spending a couple of weeks with the Yankees in spring training working with young pitchers. Hunter is tempted by the coaching job.

Finally, he decides to stay home. He wants to spend the summer with his kids, and he figures that his entire salary as pitching coach would go to pay someone to run the farm while he was away. Catfish calls Yogi to thank him for the offer, and wishes him luck.

Hunter will, however, play baseball again this summer—with

As for Hundhammer, he never found a groove during the 1983 season. With his new wife, Linda, who moved north to spend the summer with him, Hundy bounced back and forth between the Pawtucket and New Britain Red Sox. (The Class AA team had moved from Bristol to better facilities in nearby New Britain.) He also split his time between two positions, second and third base.

Hundhammer had a disappointing season, at bat and in the field. He finished with a .223 batting average, with nine home runs, and 45 RBIs in 390 at-bats. He also committed 23 errors.

He began the 1984 season in Pawtucket, determined to improve. He started well, batting .285 through the team's first 60 games. Now 25, Hundhammer knows that this season will be a make-or-break year for him. He says, "If I come back and don't do well . . . count me out of being in the big leagues."

Shortly after 8 P.M. on September 6, 1982, Ron Darling took the mound for the New York Mets to face the Philadelphia Phillies at Shea Stadium. It was his first major league game.

Darling began in dramatic fashion, striking out the first two batters he faced—future Hall of Famers Joe Morgan and Pete Rose. He went on to retire the next seven men in order.

In the sixth inning, though, Darling made a couple of costly mistakes. He walked Morgan and committed two balks, allowing a run to score. Trailing 1–0, Darling left the game in the seventh and was charged with the hard-luck loss.

Darling continued to pitch well—and to lose—in his September tryout. He finally got his first major league win in his last start of the season against Pittsburgh, going the distance in a 4–2 victory. He finished with a 1–3 record and a 2.80 ERA in 35 innings.

As the 1984 season began, Darling had won a spot in the Mets' rotation. He showed signs of improvement as the season unfolded and his record stood at 8–3 in late June. Darling had become an important member of an improving young Mets team.

Ron Kittle was at home with his parents in Gary on the night of November 22, 1983, when the phone rang. It was a caller from the Baseball Writers of America, telling him that he had been elected the American League's Rookie of the Year.

"It's a special moment for me," he said, "something you can only experience once in a lifetime." It was a fitting end to an outstanding rookie year.

Kittle finished 1983 with 35 home runs and 100 RBIs for the division champion Chicago White Sox. His power totals are even more impressive when you realize that he batted sixth for most of the season and came to the plate 100 times fewer than, say, Jim Rice, who led the league in homers with 39.

Kittle never did lick his nemesis—the strikeout—as he led the league in that category with 150. His batting average tailed off to .254 in the second half of the season, and his fielding remained suspect.

Still, the White Sox brass was obviously delighted with the budding young star. In the spring of 1984, Chicago signed Kittle to a three-year contract starting at $175,000 a year. With bonuses and raises, the contract could eventually bring him $1 million.

Despite his solid season in 1983, Bill Almon had little hope of winning a job as an everyday player in 1984. The Oakland A's, in fact, added several players to their roster during the winter who would probably make it harder for him to break into the lineup.

The A's signed free agents Joe Morgan, Bruce Bochte, and Dave Kingman, and they gave the shortstop job to Donnie Hill. After Oakland's first 63 games, Almon had come to bat only 55 times and was hitting just .164.

Steve Kemp reported to spring training in good spirits as the New York Yankees prepared for the 1984 season with their new manager, Yogi Berra. Not surprisingly, Kemp was pleased to see Billy Martin go; he was among the players to appear at the news conference when Berra's signing was announced.

The first day of spring training, Berra sought out Kemp, knowing that the outfielder had been troubled by Martin's refusal to stick with him last year. "You're going to be playing left field for me every day," Berra said.

Kemp was pleased. "I'm not saying I'll go out there to do well just for Yogi. But it's nice to know the manager is behind you, and it's nice to know he isn't about to get all over you and sit you down if you don't get a hit."

Kemp had another reason to be pleased. His eyesight was virtually back to normal, and he was hitting the ball well all spring.

Kemp's season began on an ominous note. He pulled a groin muscle during an exhibition game and was placed on the disabled list after playing only one inning on Opening Day.

Not long after returning from the injury, though, Kemp began to hit the ball with authority. He lifted his batting average to over .300 and, for the moment at least, seemed to have regained his confidence.

Ferguson Jenkins was given his release by the Chicago Cubs in March 1984, two weeks after the beginning of spring training. He was not signed by another team and planned to spend the summer on his farm in Blenheim, Ontario.

Jenkins had wanted to pitch one more season in the big leagues, and he still hoped to win 300 games. But the Chicago team was building for its future, and he was a reminder of a not-so-happy Cub past.

The Cubs' brass doubted that he could pitch anymore and complained about his attitude. On the first day of spring workouts, for example, Jenkins claimed his equipment wasn't ready and went back to the hotel without telling anybody. New manager Jim Frey wasn't happy, saying, "I don't think he showed the right respect for me, [general manager] Dallas Green, or the players."

Jenkins, 40, took his release in stride. He expressed the hope that some other team would offer him a job. But he also said he welcomed the chance to spend more time with his family. "Maybe it's time to take the easy way out and go home," he said.

Bill White had an enjoyable winter, spending two weeks in Sarajevo, Yugoslavia, to cover the Winter Olympics for ABC Radio. He began his fourteenth season as a broadcaster for the Yankees in the spring of 1984.

Jim Hunter spent a month with the Yankees in spring training, working with their young pitchers. Then he returned home to Hertford to prepare for the spring planting of corn, soybeans, and peanuts.

# BASEPATHS

## *From the Minor Leagues to the Majors and Beyond*

## MARC GUNTHER

**BASEPATHS: From the Minor Leagues to the Majors and Beyond**
*Marc Gunther*. Scribners, $14.95 ISBN 0-684-18175-4
In an ingeniously structured book, *Hartford* (Conn.) *Courant* staffer Gunther writes of nine current and former baseball players, all archetypes of players at particular stages in their careers. He opens with a 21-year-old first baseman playing his first professional game in the Appalachian League, moves to two young men seasoned in the minors who may make it to the top, and to Ron Darling of the Tidewater Tides, certain to move up. Next come Ron Kittle of the White Sox, rookie of the year in 1983, Bill Almon of Oakland, a utility player worried about hanging on in the majors, and Steve Kemp, a star. Finally there are Ferguson Jenkins, his career on the downhill slide, Bill White, who left the diamond for the broadcast booth, and Catfish Hunter, who has returned to the farming life he likes best. With admirable economy, Gunther covers the entire sport and fans will enjoy his book immensely.

--Publishers Weekly

Publication Date: October 31, 1984
Price: $14.95

Charles Scribner's Sons · New York